高等院校经济与管理专业教材

现代国际商务函电

主　编　喆　儒
副主编　杨玉珺　周晓俭　李媛媛

人民邮电出版社

北　京

图书在版编目（CIP）数据

现代国际商务函电 / 喆儒主编. —北京：人民邮
电出版社，2011.4
高等院校经济与管理专业教材
ISBN 978-7-115-25048-3

I. ①现… II. ①喆… III. ①国际贸易—英语—电报
信函—写作—高等学校—教材 IV. ①H315

中国版本图书馆CIP数据核字（2011）第037189号

内容提要

本书全面介绍了企业在现代国际商务活动中与客户进行业务往来时撰写英文商务信函的基本格式与写作原则，并涵盖了外贸业务的各个环节，如建立业务关系、询盘、报盘和还盘、回复报盘、订单及执行、支付、装运、保险、投诉、索赔、理赔及代理等。

本书从实用的角度出发，列举了众多真实的合同和单证范例，并对其进行了详细讲解和分析，有利于加深学生对外贸业务实际操作的理解和对知识的灵活运用。

本书适用于高等院校国际贸易专业教学和企业相关人员的业务技能培训。

高等院校经济与管理专业教材
现代国际商务函电

◆ 主　编　喆 儒
　　副 主 编　杨玉珺　周晓俭　李媛媛
　　责任编辑　李宝琳
　　执行编辑　代新梅

◆ 人民邮电出版社出版发行　　　北京市崇文区夕照寺街14号
　　邮编　100061　　电子邮件　315@ptpress.com.cn
　　网址　http://www.ptpress.com.cn
　　北京鑫正大印刷有限公司印刷

◆ 开本：787×1092　1/16
　　印张：15.5　　　　　　　　　　2011年4月第1版
　　字数：150千字　　　　　　　　2011年4月北京第1次印刷

ISBN 978-7-115-25048-3
定　价：28.00元
读者服务热线：（010）67129879　印装质量热线：（010）67129223
反盗版热线：（010）67171154

前　言

　　商务函电是国际贸易专业的核心课程之一，是一门将英语技能与外贸业务相结合的课程，学生既要具备扎实的英语基础，又要掌握基本的外贸业务知识，以提高在英语文化背景下的商务知识应用能力和多元文化下的商务沟通能力。学习本课程的前提是要求学生已经具备一定的英语写作能力，并且了解基本的进出口业务知识。

　　随着国际贸易日新月异的发展，原有的商务沟通方式和渠道也在不断发生变化，为了更好地适应国际贸易专业学生和外贸从业人员的需求，有必要根据我国外贸实践的新发展和新趋势对商务函电教材进行重新编排。作者编写本书的目的就是希望帮助相关人员在学习和工作中掌握书写商务函电的技巧和方法，锻炼娴熟的英语书面表达能力，并促使其认识到良好的沟通和交际能力在商务活动中的重要性。

　　本书共分为十四章。第一章详细介绍了正式英文商务信函的基本格式和写作原则；第二章至第十二章介绍了外贸业务中各类商务函电的具体写法，并对相关范例及重要词句进行了介绍和讲解；第十三章至第十四章介绍了近年来在外贸业务中普遍应用的商务传真与电子邮件的写作要点，以及其他商务文书，如备忘录及会议记录的写作要点和规范。书中除第一章介绍商务信函的格式与结构之外，其余各章基本都包括了写作要点、范例讲解、实用例句和练习题四个模块，格式工整、结构清晰，有利于学生循序渐进地掌握各章知识点。

　　本书由喆儒担任主编，杨玉珺、周晓俭、李媛媛担任副主编，由于编写时间较为仓促，加之作者水平有限，书中难免有不足之处，敬请读者批评指正。

目　录

第一章　商务信函的结构与格式（Structure and Format of English Business Letters）·················1

第一节　商务信函的结构（Structure of English Business Letters）············3

第二节　商务信函的格式（Format of English Business Letters）···········9

第三节　信封的写法（Addressing Envelopes）················15

第四节　商务信函的写作原则（Writing Principles）················17

第二章　建立业务联系（Establishing Business Relations）·········25

第一节　如何写作建立业务联系的商务信函（How to Write a Letter to Establish Business Relations）················27

第二节　资信调查等的范例讲解（Sample Letters on Credit Investigation and Establishing Business Relations）················29

第三节　建立业务联系的实用例句（Useful Sentences on Establishing Business Relations）················35

第三章　询盘（Inquiry）················41

第一节　询盘的写作要点（Introduction on How to Inquire）············43

第二节　询盘的范例讲解（Sample Letters on Inquiries）···········44

第三节　询盘的实用例句（Useful Sentences on Inquiring）···········49

第四章　报盘和还盘（Offers and Counter Offers）················55

第一节　报盘和还盘的写作要点（How to Write an Offer and a Counter Offer）················57

第二节　报实盘和还盘的范例讲解（Sample Letters on Firm Offer and Counter Offer）················59

1

第三节 报盘的实用例句（Useful Sentences on Offering）·················64

第五章 回复报盘（Reply on Offers）·················69

第一节 回复报盘的写作要点（Introduction on How to Reply an Offer）···71

第二节 接受和拒绝报盘的范例讲解（Sample Letters on Accepting and Declining Offers）·················71

第三节 回复报盘的实用例句（Useful Sentences on a Reply to Offer）···75

第六章 订单及执行（Orders and Their Fulfillment）·················79

第一节 订单的写作要点（Introduction on Order）·················81

第二节 下订单的范例讲解（Sample Letters on Placing Orders）·········82

第三节 有关订单的实用例句（Useful Sentences on Orders）·············86

第七章 购货合同及销售确认书（Purchase Contract and Sales Confirmation）·················93

第一节 合同的写作要点（Introduction on Contracts）·················95

第二节 合同及销售确认书的范例讲解（Sample Letters on Contracts and S/C）·················99

第三节 订立合同的实用例句（Useful Sentences for Entering into a Contract）·················103

第八章 支付（Payment）·················109

第一节 支付与信用证的写作要点（Introduction on Payment and L/C）···111

第二节 支付术语和信用证的信函范例（Sample Letters Regarding to Payment Terms and L/C）·················121

第三节 信用证和汇票的实用例句（Useful Sentences on L/C and Bill of Exchange）·················131

第九章 装运（Shipment） ·······137

第一节 装运的写作要点（Introduction on Shipment） ·······139

第二节 装运实务的范例讲解（Sample Letters on Shipment） ·······140

第三节 提单和装箱单范本（Samples of B/L and Packing List） ·······145

第十章 保险（Insurance） ·······151

第一节 保险的写作要点（Introduction on Insurance） ·······153

第二节 保险实务的范例讲解（Sample Letters on Insurance Practices） ·······157

第三节 保险单的实用例句（Useful Sentences on Insurance Policy） ·······161

第十一章 投诉、索赔和理赔（Complaint, Claim and Settlement） ·······167

第一节 索赔与回复的写作要点（Introduction on Claim and Its Reply） ·······169

第二节 索赔与理赔的范例讲解（Sample Letters on Claim and Its Acceptance） ·······170

第三节 索赔的实用例句（Useful Sentences Related to Claims） ·······178

第十二章 代理（Agency） ·······185

第一节 代理的写作要点（Introduction on Agency） ·······187

第二节 销售代理的范例讲解（Sample Letters on Selling Agency） ·······188

第三节 代理协议书的实用例句（Useful Sentences on Agency Agreement） ·······197

第十三章 商务传真与电子邮件（Fax and E-mail） ·······203

第一节 商务传真与电子邮件的写作要点（Introduction on Fax and E-mail） ·······205

第二节 商务传真与电子邮件的范例讲解（Samples of Fax and E-mail） ·······213

第三节　商务传真与电子邮件的实用例句（Useful Sentences on Fax and E-mail）……………………………………………………219

第十四章　其他商务文书（Other Business Documents ）………223

第一节　备忘录及会议记录的写作要点（Introduction on Memo and Minutes of Meeting）………………………………………225

第二节　备忘录及会议记录的范例讲解（Sample Letters on Memos and Minutes of Meeting）………………………………227

第三节　备忘录及会议记录的实用例句（Useful Sentences on Memo and Minutes of Meeting）…………………………………233

第一章 商务信函的结构与格式

Structure and Format of English Business Letters

本章内容提要
本章包括商务信函的书写结构、格式、写作原则，以及信封的写法。

本章知识重点
商务信函的结构和基本格式。

第一节　商务信函的结构
（Structure of English Business Letters）

商务信函的写作目的是为了帮助企业进行内外部沟通，如从潜在客户那里获取信息，与媒体接触以便为产品或服务宣传，为客户提供有关新产品或服务的信息，与求职者联系或向员工通告重要事项。虽然由于更为快捷的电子邮件的产生，使得商务信函在当今国际贸易实务中的应用已远远不如从前频繁，但是在相当多的场合下，一封书写规范、措辞得体的商务信函往往是十分必要的，甚至会给企业带来意想不到的业务机会和树立良好的形象。

写好英文商务信函不仅要求学生掌握相关的业务知识，熟悉外贸流程和法规、惯例，具备相应的语言基础，还要了解商务信函的写作结构、格式与行文特点。

商务信函的结构可分为基本部分（Main parts）与附加部分（Additional parts）。

一、基本部分

基本部分是一封正式的商务信函不可缺少的部分，包括信头（Letter head）、发信日期（Date）、封内名称和地址（Inside name and address）、称呼（Salutation）、正文（Body of the letter）、结尾敬语（Complimentary close）和签名（Signature）（包括手写和打印）。

1. 信头

信头是信笺上（多为顶端正中）事先印制好的有关发信人（Sender）的信息，包括企业名称（Firm's name）、地址（Address）、传真号码（Fax）、电子邮箱（E-mail）、电话号码（Telephone number）、公司微标（Logo），甚至经营范围（Line of business）和创立年份（Year of establishment）等。如果信笺上没有印制好的信头，发信人应将相应内容打印在信笺上面，其位置视具体格式而定。如商务信函采用完全齐头式（Full-block form），信头应自左边起笔；如采用缩行式（Indented form）、改良齐头式（Modified-block form）或半齐头式（Semi-block form），则一般将信头排在中间。

Illustration of Letter head

×× United Import and Export Co., LTD

Add: Suite 505, Entrance B, ×× Plaza, 28 An Ding Men East Street,

Dongcheng District, Beijing, P.R. China, 100007

Phone: (0086)-10-84321234   Fax: (0086)-10-84321235

E-mail: info@××.com.cn   Website: www. ××.com.cn

---

2. 发信日期

商务信函务必要写明发信日期，其位置一般在信头最后一行的下面两行至四行的地方。采用齐头式的商务信函，日期自左边齐头开始；而采用其他格式的商务信函，日期可放在该行右边，最后一个数字与正文的右边距对齐。

日期有两种写法：（1）October 10, 2010（美式）；（2）10th October 2010（英式）。在这里需要注意的是，前者的日与年之间加逗号，后者的月与年易于分辨，不必加逗号，且日可用序数词也可用基数词；无论哪种写法都不要使用月份的缩写，也不可用数字标示月份，以免混淆。例如，以下不规范的写法就容易混淆：12-10-2010、12/10/2010、12/10/10，这一日期在美国代表2010年12月10日，在欧洲大部分国家却表示2010年10月12日。

3. 封内名称和地址

收信人的名称和地址除了出现在信封上之外，还必须写在信的内文中，目的是确保信会送抵收信人手中以及便于存档。此部分通常置于日期之下两行或四行的地方，依次按顺序包括如下内容。

（1）收信人姓名（Name of addressee）。

（2）收信人的头衔与职位（Title of addressee）。

（3）单位名称（Name of organization）。

（4）地址（Full address）。

需要注意的是，封内名称和地址的内容与格式应与信封上完全一致。商务信函如有具体的收信人姓名，在其之前一定要加上适当尊称，如Mr., Miss., Dr.；如收信人有职位时，可将其职位直接置于人名之后，也可放在人名的下一行，如下例。

Dr. Thomas Bauer

Vice President

Dortmund Trading Co., Ltd

收信人地址写在单位名称下一行，通常分作三行。地址的顺序与中文习惯相反，依次为门牌号码（门牌号码前不加"No."或"#"）、街道名称，城市、州/省、邮编，寄达国名称，如下例。

24 Broadway

New York, NY 100021

U.S.A

4. 称呼

称呼是在进入正文前，写信人对收信人的敬称，相当于中文书信中的敬启者。称呼的位置在封内名称和地址下面两行的地方，并与左边靠齐。称呼的开首字母及头衔必须大写，例如，Dear Sir不能写成Dear sir；Dear Doctor Chang不能写成Dear doctor Chang。

如果发信人知道收信人的名字，最好称呼他们的头衔或姓，男性称Mr.，女性称Ms.。如果知道对方是已婚女士，就称Mrs.，未婚称Miss。但是Mr.，Ms.，Mrs.，Miss等不能单独作为称呼，后面必须有姓，如Dear Mr. Chang，Dear Ms. Ford。如果不知道收信人的姓名，可以用Dear Sir or Madam；如果收信人是公司内不特定的人，则用复数形式的称呼，如Dear Sirs（英式），Gentlemen（美式）或Dear Mesdames。称呼后面一定要有标点，可用","（英式）或"；"（美式）。

5. 正文

一封信的正文就是信的主体，也是最重要的部分，其位置在称呼或者主要事由的下面两行。视内容繁简，正文通常可分为若干合理的短段落，分别作为开头、中间部分和结尾。对于内容较少的信，可以在段与段之间采用双行距（Double line spacing），对于内容较长的信可以采用单行距（Single line spacing），但是收信人和发信人的地址任何时候都应采用单行距。正文分段时要注意，一段应该只表达一个意思，甚至为了便于归档或处理，一封信最好只围绕一个主题。

正文要简洁、明晰、礼貌，同时还要做到语法规范、拼写无误、标点正确。

开头语一般自成一段，可以简单地说明写信的原因或要求，并提及相关的合同、信用证、提单等文件。如果是与客户第一次通信，发信人一定要简要地介绍自己；如果是在回复对方的来信，一定要提到对方来信的日期和主要事由。正文中间部分的内容如果太多，可以使用小标题；如果一个段落中包含几个要点，可以用项目编号或符号来加以突出。总之，中间部分设计得当会使得信看上去美观大方。结尾部分要另起一段，通常会重复一下信的主旨，起到强调或提醒的作用，或是表达良好的祝愿和希望等。

当正文内容较长，需要两页或两页以上篇幅时，应在续页上注明收信人名称、页数、日期。如果前页已将正文内容写完，只剩下签名或结尾敬语时应作适当调整，要么加大行距，将前页的部分内容转至续页，要么缩减内容或省去主要事由，将结尾敬语和签名等都压缩至前页。续页写法见以下两例。

（1）Mr. Thomas Bauer

　　　Page 2

　　　October 10, 2010

（2）Page 2

　　　The ABC Company　　　　　　October 10, 2010

6. 结尾敬语

结尾敬语是正文内容结束后的客气话，类似于中文的"此致，敬礼"、"顺颂商祺"等含义，其位置在正文的下面两行，第一个字母需大写。如用齐头式，应从左边齐头开始；在其他格式中，则放在该行的右边。

常用的较为正式的结尾敬语有：Yours faithfully, Faithfully yours, Yours truly, Truly yours；与收信人有过交往的可用：Yours sincerely, Sincerely yours；更为亲切的有：Cordially yours, Yours cordially；表示特别尊敬的（例如自荐信、下属写给上司）有：Yours respectfully, Yours very respectfully, Respectfully yours。

7. 签名

签名一般包含三个部分：寄信人的姓名、职务头衔及签名，但更常用的是包含四个部分的签名，即还要在结尾敬语的下面写上寄信人所属公司或机构的名称。寄信人手写签名以示对信件负责；而手写签名往往难于辨认，所以签名的下面一定要将发信人的姓名和职务等打印出来。一般在结尾敬语（或公司名称）和打印签名之间空三行，留出手写签名的地方，如下例。

Yours truly,

Benjamin Gunn（手写签名）

Benjamin Gunn

 Sales Manager

GLOBAL TRADING COMPANY

如果是秘书代老板签字，可以用下面的格式。

Sincerely yours,

Joe King（手写签名）

Joe king

Secretary to Mr. Jack Jones

注意：签名忌用图章，且最好始终保持一种风格，并且使用墨水笔而不是圆珠笔。

二、附加部分

一封信除了上述基本部分之外，还有一些需要附加的特别事项。商务信函中常见的附加事项有查询号（Reference number）、注意事项（Attention line）、事由（Subject line）、附件（Enclosure）、抄送（Carbon copy notation）及附言（Postscript）等。

1. 查询号

公司为了便于往来书信的存档和查阅，有时需要给每一封信都编有查询号，也叫案号，并在回信时提到彼此的查询号。查询号的位置一般在信头下面靠左边缘或右边缘，或与日期平行靠左的位置，有时也放在信末寄信人签名的下面一行靠左的位置。常用的形式有：

Our Ref. TB/JJ

Your Ref. JJ/TB

Ref.20100401TB

2. 注意事项

如果收信人是某个机构，但发信人希望某个人或者某个特定部门注意到该信，可以加上经办人，位置通常在封内名称和地址以及称呼之间靠左，或者与称呼在同一行居中，如下例。

Attention: Mr. Franz Jorg

Attention of Mr. Franz Jorg

Attn: Sales Department

3. 事由

为了让收信人对信的内容一目了然，提高办公效率，可以在信中标明事由或主题。事由一般是信函的主题，放在称呼与正文之间，全部大写，字体加粗或加下划线以示强调。其表现方式如下。

（1）Dear Sirs,

Subject: YOUR ORDER NO.123

（2）Dear Sirs,

YOUR ORDER NO.123

（3）Dear Sirs,

Re: **YOUR ORDER NO.123**

4. 附件

如果随信附寄了东西，发信人应在正文中提及，并在签名下面空一行的位置注明，以提请收信人注意。如果附寄的文件等不止一份，还要相应编码，以便收信人识别，其表现方式如下。

Enclosure

Encl.

Enclosures

Encls.

Enclosure: as stated

Enclosures: 2

Enclosure：one price list

5. 抄送

如果发信的同时需要将副本抄送给他人或相关单位，以"C.C."为标记置于附件的下面靠左，如下例。

C.C.: Beijing Office, GLOBAL TRADING COMPANY

C.C. to Beijing Office, GLOBAL TRADING COMPANY

6. 附言

如果写信人在写完信之后想起来补充一件事或是强调一些内容，可以在抄送的下面空一行写上"P.S."符号，作用相当于中文的"再启"、"又及"等，然后将需要追加的内容加在后面。需要注意的是，除非时间关系不便重写，一般应尽量避免使用附言，如下例。

Encl: a/s

C.C.: New York Corp.

P.S.: The samples will be mailed to you tomorrow.

第二节 商务信函的格式
(Format of English Business Letters)

商务信函的外观和格式非常重要，有些公司会规定采用固定的某种格式；有时写信人也可以根据自己的习惯选择适当的格式。常见的商务信函有以下四种基本格式：完全齐头式、改良齐头式、半齐头式和缩行式。美国最常用的是完全齐头式和半齐头式，而缩行式已经略显老套。

一、完全齐头式

这种完全齐头式（Full-block style）格式现在使用范围广泛，因为它不仅快捷、高效，而且能反映进行商业活动的积极性。信件的所有内容都从左边顶格开始，排列整齐，不向右缩进。这一格式的优点是写信人在打字时不必考虑第一行缩进的问题，节省时间；缺点是页面有时看上去失去平衡。

正文的第一段与称呼间隔一行，段落内行距为单行距，段落之间行距为双行距。详见下例。

Innov Imp & Exp Co., Ltd

77 Eastern Road

Chiswick, London

UK

Telephone: 45632

Fax: 68539

26th July 2010

ABC Stores Plc.

8 High Street

Manchester

Dear Sirs,

It has just come to our attention that you have lately opened your new American headquarter in New York. Congratulations on your bold venture.

As you know, our company have had a long business association in the UK. We look forward to collaborating with you in your American venture. Please let us know if we could be of any assistance to you. We will be delighted to help.

We wish you the very best of luck and a prosperous future.

Yours faithfully,

Sandra Jones

Sales Manager

二、改良齐头式

改良齐头式（Modified-block style）是在齐头式的基础上加以改进，正文同样是每一行都从左边顶格开始，但是日期、结尾敬语和签名却放在右边对齐，这样可以兼顾省时与平衡。详见下例。

Innov Imp & Exp Co., Ltd

77 Eastern Road

Chiswick, London

UK

Telephone: 45632

Fax: 68539

Your Ref.:20100101   26th July 2010

Mr. Pierre Dupont

Managing Director

Dupont Freres

4 Rue de la Paix

Paris 16

France

Dear Mr. Dupont,

Subject: OFFER OF THE SUMMER DISCOUNT OF 20％

I enjoyed touring your company last week. Thank you so much for giving me the opportunity to demonstrate the new Handi-Jack tool belt.

I checked with the distribution center about your enquiry on bulk orders. Yes, I can still offer you the summer discount of 20% off each large business shipment. (Offer expires December 31, 2010.)

I look forward to hearing from you.

Yours faithfully,

Sandra Jones

Sales Manager

三、半齐头式

半齐头式（Semi-block style）有时也称作混合式在此格式中，发信人的地址是置于信的上方中间位置的。封内地址、姓名和称呼都采用齐头式，从左边开始；日期、结尾敬语和签名都在右下方。正文可以采用缩行式也可采用齐头式，即每段开首可以缩进若干字母也可以顶格写。这一格式的优点是看上去较平衡；缺点是打字有些费时。详见下例。

Innov Imp & Exp Co., Ltd

77 Eastern Road

Chiswick, London

UK

Telephone: 45632

Fax: 68539

Your Ref.: 20100101   26th July 2010

Global Trading Company

6 Feuerbach Street

Bochum

Germany

Dear Sirs,

Thank you for your enquiry of November 9, 2010. In reply, we would like to make the following offer, subject to our final confirmation:

USD15.40 per set FOB London net for Model A

USD16.80 per set FOB London net for Model B

Under separate cover, we have sent you samples of various sizes, our catalogue and price list.

If you find our offer acceptable, please fax us for confirmation.

Yours faithfully,

Sandra Jones

Sales Manager

Enc.3

　　1. Samples of various sizes

　　2. Catalogue

　　3. Price list

C.C.: Mr. N Brown（Purchasing Manager）

四、缩行式

缩行式（Indented style）的特点是把信头置于中间，日期、结尾敬语和签名放在右边，正文每个段落首行缩进4~6个字母。这种格式的优点是美观、对称；缺点是写作费时。详见下例。

Innov Imp & Exp Co., Ltd

77 Eastern Road

Chiswick, London

UK

Telephone: 45632

Fax: 68539

26th November 2010

Ms Fiona Green

Moda Fashions Inc.

665 Fifth Avenue

New York

USA

Dear Ms Green,

Thank you for your enquiry of 19th November, 2010 for our electric tools.

We are now sending our quotation sheet for your selection. We also enclose 2 samples and are sure that you will be satisfied with their superior quality.

Hope to serve you soon.

Yours sincerely,

Sandra Jones

Sales Manager

Enclosures

第三节　信封的写法
（Addressing Envelopes）

信封上记载的内容通常有：发信人名称和地址（Return address）、收信人名称和地址（Mailing address）、邮寄指示（Mailing direction）和注意事项（Remarks）等，但这些内容在寄往国外信函信封上的摆放，位置不同于国内信封的写法。

一、发信人名称和地址

发信人名称和地址写在信封的左上角，一些商务机构所用的信封通常已经在左上角印好了发信人地址。

二、收信人名称和地址

收信人名称和地址写在信封中央偏下的位置，其写法、标点符号、格式等应与封内姓名和地址保持一致。需要转交（In care of，c/o）时，将c/o放在收信人姓名下面一行转交人姓名之前，如下例。

Dr. Thomas Bauer

c/o Tania Muller

Vice President

×× Trading Co., Ltd

三、邮寄指示

邮寄指示用于指示下列事项：航空信（Via airmail）、快件（Express）或限时专递（Special delivery）等。

四、注意事项

注意事项在信封的左下方，可能是一项，也可能是多项。常见的注意事项包括以下几点。

Attention of Mr. Thomas Bauer	专呈托马斯·鲍尔先生
Kindness（or by courtesy）of Tania Muller	烦请塔尼亚·穆勒转交
Confidential	机密
Urgent	急件
Registered mail（Registered）	挂号信
Private	私函（仅限收信人亲启）
Printed matter	印刷品

也有将发信人地址写在信封盖（Back flap）上的，详见下列信封图示。

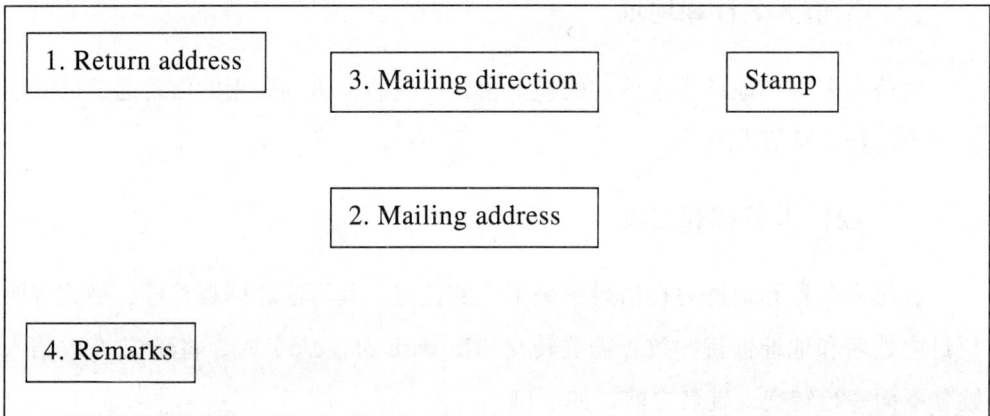

1. Return address	3. Mailing direction	Stamp
	2. Mailing address	
4. Remarks		

此外，信纸的折叠方法也非常重要，因为它可以给收信人留下最初印象。信纸的折法根据信封的大小和样式而定，但要做到美观、便于邮寄和便于收信人拆阅。

对于大型信封，信纸的折叠方法为先由下端向上端叠1/3，然后再向上叠直至与上端平齐，成三等分，然后装入信封即可。

如果是小型信封，信纸的折叠法为先由下端向上对折，再从右边向左折1/3，然后再由左向右折1/3，最后将六折的信纸装入信封中。

还有一类开窗信封（Window envelope），即在信封的中央留一个覆以透明纸的窗口。使用这种信封，折叠信纸时必须将收信人姓名和地址折于外面，使其装入信封后，收信人姓名和地址刚好可在窗口露出。使用开窗信封，无需再在信封上打印收信人的信息，可以节约时间。

第四节 商务信函的写作原则
（Writing Principles）

一封正式的商务英文信函必须具备七个要件，即7 C's Principle：完整（Completeness）、清楚（Clarity）、正确（Correctness）、具体（Concreteness）、简洁（Conciseness）、礼貌（Courtesy）以及体谅（Consideration）。

一、完整

一封商务信函应该包括所有要传达的必要信息，所以在发出之前要仔细检查，以免有所遗漏。特别是涉及外贸业务的信函一定要将相关交易条件逐一交代清楚，并且对相关信息予以完整说明，以免对方花大量时间去核实对照，如下例。

Dear Sirs,

We are returning the goods shipped, as it arrived too late.

Yours truly,

这封信意欲告知退货的事实，但是语焉不详，没有说明是哪一批货、迟交了多久、什么时间退回的，因而不是一次有效的沟通。改写后如下例。

Dear Sirs,

We are returning the cotton goods, your invoice No.123, by S.S. "Diamond" today.

This was received May 2, too late for our Spring Sale. You will find on reference to our order of January 3, on which this was to be shipped to reach us not later than March 15.

Yours faithfully,

二、清楚

商务信函措辞应明白清楚，不致引起误会。信的内容要具有连贯性、段落分明、思路清晰、排列妥当。商务信函要想清楚地表达需注意以下几点。

1. 避免使用意义不明确的词语

例如，As to the steamers sailing from Shanghai to Sydney, we have bimonthly

17

direct services. bimonthly一词既有"一个月两次"的意思，也有"两个月一次"的意思，所以用在这里不够明确，应改为下述之一。

We have two direct sailings every month from Shanghai to Sydney.

We have semi-monthly direct sailing from Shanghai to Sydney.

We have a direct sailing from Shanghai to Sydney every two months.

2. 修饰词应放在适当的位置

例1. We shall be able to supply 100 cases of the item only.

例2. We shall be able to supply 100 cases only of the item.

由于only的不同位置，使得例1的含义是以商品为限，例2是以100箱为限。可见，修饰词的位置不同，其含义也迥然不同。

3. 注意句子结构

例1. We sent you 5 samples yesterday of the goods which you requested in your letter of May 25 by air.

例2. We sent you, by air, 5 samples of the goods which you requested in your letter of May 25 yesterday.

例1强调的是寄送样品的时间是昨天，例2强调的是寄送方式为航空邮寄。

4. 使用日常用语

写作商务信函忌用生僻字、复杂的术语、俚语、土语、不通用的缩略语。如果要表示大都市，用"big city"就可以，不一定要用"metropolitan"；要表示给予，可以用"give"，不必用"render"。使用日常用语可以让读者迅速、准确地理解发信人的意思，有时也不妨使用通俗易懂的口语化语言。

此外，发信人还需注意正文段落不应太长，一段只有一个主题；尽量用简短的句子，必要时可以把长句子分成几个简单的短句子。

三、正确

正确不仅仅是指语法无误，标点和拼写准确，也包括语言规范、表述恰当、数字精确，以及商务术语使用正确。详见下例。

例1. This is the lowest price available to you.（过分夸张）

This is the lowest price we can offer you now.（正确）

例2. This fridge not only is attractive in proper price, but also in good quality.
（语法错误）

This fridge is attractive not only in proper price, but also in good quality.
（正确）

例3. 50 dozen or up; 50 dozen and upwards（50打以上）

例4. USD100 or less; USD100 and below（100美元以下）

例5. Not exceeding a total of 30 days（30天以下）

例6. On or before May 12（5月12日以前（含当日））

例7. Up to and including October 10（10月10日为止，并包括10日在内）

例8. Up to $30 inclusive（30美元为止，包括30美元）

例9. From the 2nd to the 15th of March both inclusive（从3月2日到15日，头尾包括在内）

例10.Pay in advance（预付款）；pay by installments（分期付款）；pay at sight（见票即付）；pay 90 days after sight（见票后90天付款）

四、具体

所谓具体就是要言之有物、有凭有据，切忌空泛抽象。

1. 避免抽象笼统。例如，夸赞自己货物的品质不要只说"best"、"supreme"、"fine"等，而是要将其优点一一列举出来。例如，Our apples are excellent.（不具体）；Our apples are juicy, crispy and tender.（具体）

2. 明确写出相关单据、文件的查询号。例如，We have effected shipment under your L/C.（未指出开证行和信用证号码）；We have effected shipment under your L/C No.123 issued by Bank of China.（具体）

3. 明确表示日期和期间。在日期和期间的表述上要避免使用"recent"、"in due course"、"early July"等含糊词语。例如，As requested in your recent letter we have already sent the samples to you.（不具体）；As requested in your letter dated October 10, we sent you the samples by air parcel on October 18.（具体）

五、简洁

撰写商务信函力求简洁扼要，切忌冗长，在词能达意的原则下，尽量使用简单浅显的词句。

1. 避免不必要的重复。例如，"unexpected surprise"、"grateful thanks"、"personal opinion"、"new changes"、"exactly identical"、"perfectly clear"、"true fact"等词组就是重复的用法。

2. 避免啰嗦的表达方式。例如，We wish to acknowledge receipt of your letter... （啰嗦）；可改写成：We appreciate your letter... （简洁）。类似的表达如下。

啰嗦的表达方式	简洁的表达方式
Due to the fact that	Because, as
During the time that	While
Few and far between	Seldom
For the reason that	Since, because
For the purpose of	For, to
In view of the fact that	Because
In the event that	If
At your early convenience	Early
In advance of, prior to, previous to	Before
At an early date	Soon, early
With reference to, with regard to	About
In spite of the fact that	Although
In the near future	Soon
In regard to	To
With a view to	To
There can be no doubt that	Doubtless
In the amount of	For
At all times	Always
In accordance with	By, with

3. 使用短句子，尽量用短语代替句子，用单词代替短语。详见下例。

Mr. Jorg, who is general manager of Global Trading Company, said he would like to talk to you personally. （冗长）

Mr. Jorg, general manager of Global Trading Company, said he would like to talk to you personally.（简洁）

Please don't hesitate to call upon us.（冗长）

Please write us.（简洁）

Please give consideration to the long-term business relationship...（冗长）

Please consider the long-term business relationship...（简洁）

4. 用主动语态简化句子。一般来说，主动语态比被动语态更简洁，而且易于理解。

例如，It is noted that the sales volume has been increasing.（冗长）

改为：We noted that the sales volume has increased.（简洁）

再如，It is believed that this policy will be beneficial to our customers.（冗长）

改为：We believe this policy will benefit our customers.（简洁）

六、礼貌

商务信函要求做到谦恭有礼。在写信时应适当地运用"kindly"、"please"、"thank you"、"we have pleasure"、"We regret that"等词语。无论是索赔、投诉、质问或是拒绝对方的要求，措辞都应该力求客气委婉，切忌使用过分情绪化甚至粗鲁的语言，以免给公司和自己的形象带来不可挽回的损失。详见下例。

1. We must refuse your order.（refuse语气太强烈）

改为：We regret that we are not in a position to accept your order.（regret含有客气语意）

2. You did not enclose the cheque with your order.（主动句式有谴责对方之意）

改为：The cheque was not enclosed with your order.（改为被动语气，委婉、和缓）

3. We can not understand why you have had trouble with this article.（否定句式易引起对方不快）

改为：We are just wondering if there should be some reason for your having trouble with this article.（改为肯定语气，易博得对方好感）

4. We can not comply with your request.（不够婉转，太生硬）

改为：We are afraid we can not comply with your request.（使用婉转语法）

类似的婉转语句还有："It seems (would seem) to us"、"We might say"、

"We would suggest"、"As you may be aware" 等。

七、体谅

在撰写商务信函时，要注意设身处地地为对方着想，因此在沟通时要多用第二人称代词You/Your，而不是第一人称代词I/We/Us/Our，即所谓 "You attitude"。请比较下列表达。

"We" expression	"You" expression
We are pleased to announce that...	You will be pleased to know that...
We follow the policy because that...	You will benefit from this policy because...
As to our standing, we refer you to	As to our standing, you may address any inquiry
Bank of China...	To Bank of China...

需要注意的是，体谅和礼貌是分不开的。如果是谴责、投诉、责问的信函切忌满篇 "You"，这样很容易使交易双方矛盾升级。

练习题

1. 将下列内容按照一封商务信函的格式要求进行安排

（1）Sender's name: Global Trading Co., LTD

（2）Sender's address: 3823 56th Avenue S.W., Seattle, Washington 98116, USA

（3）Sender's telephone:（001）206 441 8600

（4）Sender's fax:（001）206 441 8601

（5）Date: ...

（6）Receiver's name: Sinotex United Import and Export Co., LTD

（7）Receiver's address: Rm. 1401, Zhong Da Plaza, 999 Dong Fang Rd, Pudong New Area, Shanghai, China

（8）Attention line: Export Dept.

（9）Salutation: Dear Sirs

（10）Subject line:

（11）Message:

（12）Complimentary close:

（13）Signature:

2. 为上题中的商务信函写作格式正确、内容完整的信封

第二章　建立业务联系

Establishing Business Relations

本章内容提要

本章内容包括如何与客户建立业务联系和对其进行资信调查。

本章知识重点

如何向潜在客户进行自我介绍，如何通过银行对潜在客户进行资信调查以及如何回复此类信函。

第一节 如何写作建立业务联系的商务信函
（How to write a Letter to Establish Business Relations）

交易开始和扩展的基础是建立业务关系，因为没有客户就没有交易。要扩展业务，就必须在巩固已有业务关系的基础上不断物色新的贸易伙伴，发展新的业务关系。一般情况下，买卖双方可通过毛遂自荐或第三者介绍结识贸易伙伴，待调查清楚贸易伙伴的资信状况、经营能力和业务范围等重要情况后再进行实质性的业务探讨。

一、与客户建立业务关系

在国际贸易中，企业寻找客户的渠道和方法很多，归纳起来大致有以下三种类型。

1. 他人介绍。企业可通过委托我国驻外使领馆的商务参赞（Commercial Counselor's Office）、代办处或国外驻华使领馆的商务参赞、代办处，国内外各种商会、银行以及与本企业有业务关系的企业介绍客户。

2. 媒体渠道。企业可利用各国商会（Chambers of Commerce）、工商团体、国内外出版的贸易名录（Trade Directory）、国内外报刊杂志上的广告，以及计算机数据库中的客户信息、资料寻找客户。

3. 会展途径。企业可通过在国内外参加或举办各种交易会（Trade Fair）、展览会等方式找到客户。

建立业务关系的信函又称为"首次征询"，通常包括以下几个方面的内容。

1. 表达愿望

首先要表达建立合作关系的愿望，说明本企业是从何处获悉对方地址和业务范围的。

2. 介绍企业

建立业务关系的阶段是买卖双方从陌生到熟悉，再到信任的阶段。只有买卖双方彼此信任才有可能达成交易，建立长期友好的合作关系。为了让潜在客户能够全面了解企业的情况，就要介绍企业，通常包括以下内容。

（1）经营范围。写信人应介绍本企业经营的产品或提供的服务。

（2）经营方式。经营方式包括一般进出口、来料来件加工装配、代理和独家代理等。

（3）企业实力。企业实力表现在资金资本状况、市场竞争力等方面。

3. 介绍产品

简述产品的特征和面向的消费群。

4. 期盼尽快回信

收到对方的来函后，要及时并且礼貌地回复，切忌置之不理。回函内容包括以下四个方面。

1. 引出对方的来函日期和编号。

2. 对对方的来函和诚意表示感谢。

3. 说明我方的态度，交代汇寄资料，如不能满足对方要求，应该婉述原因，真诚地表示歉意，为以后可能的交易留有余地。

4. 说明我方的明确打算。

二、对客户进行资信调查

寻找到潜在客户之后，企业要对其进行资信调查以确定对方的资信状况和经济能力。对客户进行资信调查的内容和范围主要包括以下五个方面。

1. 国外企业的组织机构情况。这一情况主要包括企业的性质、创建历史、内部组织机构、主要负责人及其担任的职务。

2. 政治情况。政治情况主要指企业负责人的政治背景，与政界的关系以及对我国的政治态度等。

3. 资信情况。资信情况包括企业的注册资本、财产以及资产负债情况、企业的经营作风、履约信用等。

4. 经营范围。经营范围主要是指企业生产或经营的商品和经营的性质。

5. 经营能力。经营能力主要包括企业每年的营业额、销售渠道、经营方式以及在当地和国际市场上的贸易关系等。

资信调查函主要包括以下内容。

1. 说明写信的原因，提出调查要求的目的，以使对方的调查方向更明确。

2. 提出具体的资信调查要求，即要求得到某一企业的资金情况、经营能力、商业信誉、履约情况等资料。

3.必要承诺，保证对所提供的一切资料严格保密。

4.表示感谢。

第二节　资信调查等的范例讲解
(Sample Letters on Credit Investigation and Establishing Business Relations)

一、资信调查函范例

Dear Sirs,

You are kindly requested to provide us with the information on credit and business operation of × × Import Company. The company address is × × . Please be convinced that all the materials you supply to us will be kept as confidential, for which you will not take any responsibilities.

Best Regards.

Yours truly,

二、出口商写给进口商建立业务关系的信函范例

Dear Mr. Jones,

We understood from your information posted on Alibaba.com that you are in the market for textiles. We would like to take this opportunity to introduce our company and products, with the hope that we may establish business relationship with your company in the future.

We are a ***joint venture specializing in*** the manufacture and export of textiles. For more details, please kindly find our catalog as enclosed, or please visit our company website at http:// × × .alibaba.com which includes our latest ***product line***.

If you're interest in our products, please let us know. It will be our pleasure to give you a ***quotation*** upon receipt of your detailed enquiry.

We look forward to receiving your ***enquiries*** soon.

三、进口商写给出口商建立业务关系的信函范例

Subject: Hope to Establish Business Relations

Gentlemen,

The Bank of America has recommended your company as being interested in establishing business relations with a Chinese company for the purpose of exporting various products of your country and importing Chinese manufactured goods.

We ***specialize*** in North American trade, but we have had no contract with your company. We send this E-mail to you in order to ***ascertain*** whether cooperation to the advantage of both companies could be established.Please see the attachment for the detailed introduction of our company.

We invite you to send us details and prices of such goods as you would be able to sell. We shall be glad to study the sales possibilities in our market.

On the other hand, please favor us with a list of those articles you are interested in obtaining from us, so that we might give you all the necessary information regarding supply possibilities.

Your early reply will be greatly appreciated.

Sincerely,

四、对进口商信函的回复范例

Subject: Reply to the E-mail of September 20

Gentlemen,

Thank you for your E-mail of September 20. We are grateful to the Bank of America for having recommended us to you. It's our pleasure to establish direct business relations with your company.

We are delighted to send you the information you need. The attached catalogue will give you full details and prices of the goods we can supply.

At present, we are interested in cotton shirts and shall be pleased if you will send us the catalogue, samples books and all necessary information on the article, so as to let us know the material and quality of your supplies.

If the quality and price offered by you is *competitive*, we would like to place large orders with you.

We await your information with interest.

Faithfully yours,

五、重要词句

1. Joint Venture 合资公司

中国境内的合资公司是经我国有关部门批准，遵守我国相关法规规定，从事某种经营活动，由一个或一个以上的国外投资方与我国投资方共同经营或独立经营，实行独立核算、自负盈亏的经济实体。具体来说，合资公司是指外国公司、企业和其他经济组织或个人，按照平等互利的原则，经我国政府批准，在我国境内，同我国的公司、企业或其他经济组织共同投资、共同经营、共担风险、共负盈亏而从事某种经营活动的企业。它的组织形式为有限责任公司。

e.g. That joint venture mainly deals in the textile products made in China.

那家合资公司主要经营中国的纺织产品。

Joint Venture shall pay taxes in accordance with the relevant laws of the People's Republic of China.

合营企业必须按照中华人民共和国的相关法律纳税。

2. specialize in / be specialized in 专门经营；专门从事

e.g. We specialize in manufacturing arts and crafts and their export trade.

我公司主要经营工艺品的生产和出口业务。

We are specialized in the manufacturing automobile parts and industry parts.

我们专业生产汽车零部件和工业部件。

The firm specializes in printing advertisements.

这家公司专门印刷广告。

3. enclose v. 随函附上

e.g. We enclose a copy of our pricelist.

随函寄去我方价目表一份。

We enclose a pamphlet illustrated the scope of our business for your reference.

随信附寄介绍我公司经营范围的小册子一份，以供参考。

We enclose our latest price list No. 12 on art goods, for which there are regular demands on your market.

随函寄上我方工艺品最新的第12号价格单，贵方市场对此有经常性的需求。

4. catalog n. 商品目录；型录

商品目录是零售企业根据企业的销售目标，把经营的商品品种用一定的书面形式，并经过一定的程序固定下来，成为企业制订商品购销计划及组织购销活动的主要依据。它是零售企业在商品经营范围内确定商品品种结构的进一步具体化和规模化，一般包括经营商品目录和必备商品目录。

e.g. Please send us your sample, catalog and price list.

请贵公司寄送样品、型录及价目表。

Please quote us your price for 100 units of Item 6 in your catalog.

请给我们提供你们产品目录上100组6号产品的报价。

For most of the articles in the catalog, we have an ample supply. All the articles displayed here are available. Generally speaking, we can supply from stock.

对于目录中的大多数产品，我们都有充足的货源。这里所有展示的商品都可供货。总体来说，我们有存货供应。

5. product line 生产线；产品系列；产品线

产品线是指一群相关的产品，这类产品可能功能相似，销售给同一顾客群，经过相同的销售途径，或者在同一价格范围内。如果能够确定产品线的最佳长度，就能为企业带来最大利润。

e.g. They have a specialized product line .

他们拥有一条专用生产线。

Based on our wide range product line and flexible production capacity, we can fulfill all of your demand and offer you with prompt services.

本公司以涵盖广泛的产品线、弹性灵活的生产力满足您的全部需求并提供快捷的服务。

These two common characteristics of the product line is broad, big sales and widely distributed.

这一产品系列的两大共同特点是销售量大并且行销地区广。

6. quotation n. 报价

在国际或国内贸易中，买方向卖方询问商品价格，卖方通过考虑自己的产品成本、利润、市场竞争力等因素，报出可行的价格。一般报价的业务流程为成本核算——制作打印报价单——上呈签署——告知客户。

e.g. Thank you for your quotation for the refrigerators.

感谢你方寄来的电冰箱报价。

7. enquiry n. 询价

e.g. We shall be pleased to receive your enquiry for machinery made in Britain.

我们很高兴收到贵公司有关英国产机器的询价。

Please quote us for the goods listed in the enclosed enquiry sheet and give your price of CIF Jakarta.

请报所附询价单上的货物价格，我们需要雅加达的到岸价。

Samples and quotations at favorable prices will be sent to you upon receipt of your specific enquiry.

一旦收到你方的具体询价，我们会马上寄送样品并报最优惠的价格。

8. ascertain v. 确定

e.g. Reviews production schedules to ascertain product data such as types, quantities, and specifications of products and scheduled delivery dates in order to plan department operations.

做好部门运作计划，审查生产订单或进度表，以确定产品类型、数量、规格和交货期等产品数据。

Consumer surveys are designed to help ascertain whether or not a product will be successful on the market.

消费者调查表的设计有助于确定一件产品在市场上成功与否。

9. competitive adj. 比赛的；竞争的；

e.g. With excellent production techniques, they were able to gain the competitive edge.

凭借极好的生产技术，他们能够取得竞争上的优势。

Maybe we could have your company as our partner for supplying us quality and price competitive products.

也许你方可以成为我们的合作伙伴，为我方提供高质量、价格合理的产品。

Accurate positioning strategy, products packaging design in line with the consumer psychology, can help enterprises in many competitive brands stand out.

市场定位准确、符合消费者心理的产品包装设计，能帮助企业在众多竞争品牌中脱颖而出。

第三节　建立业务联系的实用例句
(Useful Sentences on Establishing Business Relations)

以下是一些非常实用的关于建立业务联系的例句。

1. We have heard from China Council for the Promotion of International Trade that you are in the market for electric appliances.

   从中国国际贸易促进会获悉，你们有意采购电器产品。

2. We've come to know your name and address from the Commercial Counselor's Office of the Chinese Embassy in London.

   我们从中国驻伦敦大使馆的商务参赞处得知你们的名字和地址。

3. By the courtesy of Mr. Black, we are given to understand the name and address of your firm.

   承蒙布莱克先生的介绍，我们得知贵公司的名称和地址。

4. Your firm has been introduced（recommended, passed on） to us by Maple Company.

   枫叶公司向我方介绍了贵公司。

5. We are willing to enter into business relations with your firm.

   我们愿意与贵公司建立业务关系。

6. We now avail ourselves of this opportunity to write to you with a view to entering into business relations with you.

现在我们借此机会致函贵公司，希望和贵公司建立业务关系。

7. Our mutual understanding and cooperation will certainly result in important business.

我们之间的相互了解与合作必将促成今后重要的生意。

8. We are now writing you for the purpose of establishing business relations with you.

我们特此致函是想与贵方建立业务关系。

9. Your desire to establish business relations coincides with ours.

你方想同我方建立业务关系的愿望与我方是一致的。

10. We have the pleasure to introduce ourselves to you with the hope that we may have the opportunity of cooperating with you.

我们有幸自荐，盼望能有机会与贵方合作。

11. We take the liberty of writing to you with a view to doing business with you.

我们冒昧地写信以期待与贵公司建立业务关系。

12. Being specialized in the import of spare parts for automobiles, we express our desire to trade with you in this line.

作为专营汽车零部件的进口商，我方非常愿意和贵方建立业务关系。

13. We specialize in the export of Japanese Light Industrial Products and would like to trade with you in this line.

鉴于我方专营日本轻工业产品出口业务，我方愿与贵方在这方面开展贸易。

14. Your letter expressing the hope of establishing business connections with us has met with approval.

来函收悉，得知贵方愿与我方建立业务关系，我们表示同意。

15. We shall be glad to enter into business relations with you.

我们很高兴能与贵方建立业务关系。

16. We wish to establish friendly business relations with you to enjoy a share of mutually profitable business.

我方愿与你方建立友好业务关系，分享互利的交易。

17. Your E-mail expressing the hope of entering into business connection with

us has been received with thanks.

我们已收到你方希望同我方建立贸易关系的E-mail, 深表谢意。

18. We trust that you will reply to us immediately.

我们深信很快能得到贵方的答复。

19. To give you a general idea of our products, we are sending you under separate cover a catalogue together with a set of pamphlets for your reference.

为使贵方对我方产品有全面的了解，我方另函寄去一本商品名录及一套小册子以供参考。

20. Please let us have your specific enquiry if you are interested in any of the items listed in the catalogue. We shall make an offer promptly.

如贵方对目录中所列的任何产品感兴趣，请具体询价，我方将立即报价。

练习题

1. 选择合适的介词填空

（1）We have been _____ this line of business for many years. （in/on）

（2）This corporation is specialized _____ handling the import business of textiles. （in/for）

（3）We hope to establish business relations _____ you on the basis of mutual benefit. （for/with）

（4）Quotations and samples will be sent to you _____ receipt of your enquiries. （upon/in）

（5）We are delighted to answer your request for information on our goods _____ sale. （at/for）

（6）This is our first business transaction, so both of us should be careful _____ case something unexpected happens. （on/in）

（7）We have your name and address from the Commercial Counselor's Office of the Chinese embassy _____ Ghana. （of/in）

（8）We take the liberty _____ writing to you with a view to building up business relations with your firm.（from/of）

（9）Of course this information is strictly confidential and is given _____ any responsibility on our part.（with/without）

（10）We are writing this letter to tell you the products you required fall _____ the scope of our business activities.（within/with）

2. 选择最恰当的答案填空

（1）We are willing to _____ trade relations with your company.

    A. set   B. establish   C. found   D. establishing

（2）We are looking forward to _____ .

    A. hearing from you soon   B. receive your reply soon

    C. receiving from you soon   D. you reply soon

（3）We are one of the leading exporters _____ all kinds of computers of high quality.

    A. trade in   B. trading on   C. trading in   D. trade for

（4）We _____ that with joint efforts business between us will be developed to our mutual benefit.

    A. are convince   B. convinced   C. convincing   D. are convinced

（5）We have done _____ business in this article.

    A. consider   B. considering   C. considerable   D. to consider

（6）A new branch at Beijing is a _____ corporation.

    A. state-operated   B. state operated

    C. state operating   D. state-operating

（7）Should the quality and price be found _____ , we would like to place large orders with you.

    A. compete   B. competitive   C. complete   D. competition

（8）Your company has been kindly _____ to us by Beijing Chamber of Commerce.

A. recommendation   B. recommending

C. recommended   D. recommend

（9）Buyers are trying to take _____ of the present market conditions to buy at lower prices.

A. advance   B. advice   C. advantage   D. disadvantage

（10）We wish to introduce _____ the largest exporter of fabrics of high quality.

A. that we are   B. it that we are

C. ourselves as   D. ourselves to be

3. 将下列语句翻译成英文

（1）我们从英国商会驻华办事处获悉，你们有意采购汽车零配件。

（2）我们从驻贵国的中国大使馆商务参赞处得知贵公司是纺织品的主要出口商，并获悉贵公司有意同我公司建立业务关系。

（3）得知贵公司专门经营轻工业品，我们愿意与贵公司建立业务关系。

（4）我们的生意一直做得不错，希望能与你们建立业务关系。

（5）你方要求同我方在平等互利的基础上建立贸易关系的愿望与我方的愿望一致。

（6）我公司与此地可靠的批发商有着密切的联系，能与贵公司做可观的进口业务。

（7）希望直接洽谈，以便将你公司特种经营商品引进我地市场。

（8）我们的主要业务是纺织品和手工艺品。

（9）应贵方要求，现寄上我方所有丝绸产品的最新目录和价格表。

（10）如果你们对任何一项产品询价，我们将备感荣幸。

4. 将下列内容组织成一封以求建立业务联系的商务信函

（1）我们从贵国的贸易代表团了解到贵公司是信誉良好的玩具进口商。

（2）我们是中国广东最大的玩具制造商，专门经营毛绒和电动玩具。

（3）我们愿意在平等互利、互通有无的基础上与贵公司建立业务关系。

（4）希望能收到贵公司的回信。

第三章　询盘

Inquiry

本章内容提要
本章内容为如何向客户发出询盘。

本章知识重点
区别一般询盘和具体询盘，如何要求寄送相关资料和探询商品的品质、数量、价格和交货期等。

第一节　询盘的写作要点
（Introduction on How to Inquire）

一、关于询盘的介绍

询盘也叫询价，是指交易的一方准备购买或出售某种商品，向对方询问买卖该商品有关交易条件的过程。在实际业务中，询盘只是探寻买或卖的可能性，所以不具备法律上的约束力，询盘的一方对能否达成协议不负有任何责任。由于询盘不具有法律效力，所以可作为与对方的试探性接触，询盘人可以同时向若干个交易对象发出询盘。询盘的内容可涉及价格、规格、品质、数量、包装、装运以及索取样品等，而询盘多数只是询问价格。所以，业务上常把询盘称作询价。

询盘可采用口头或书面形式，根据询问的内容可以分成两种：一种只询问价格，索取商品目录或样品，被称为一般询盘（General enquiries）；另一种询盘则包括特定商品的各项交易条件，被称为具体询盘（Specific enquiries）。根据询问者的不同，询盘也可以分为两种：一种是买方询盘，是买方主动发出的向国外厂商询购所需货物的函电。在实际业务中，询盘一般多由买方向卖方发出。在这个过程中，买方需要注意的事项有以下几个方面：（1）对多数大路货商品，应同时向不同地区、国家和厂商分别询盘，以了解国际市场行情，争取最佳贸易条件；（2）对规格复杂或项目繁多的商品，不仅要询问价格，而且需要要求对方告之详细规格、数量等，以免往返磋商、浪费时间；（3）询盘对发出人虽无法律约束力，但企业要尽量避免无购买诚意的询盘，否则容易丧失信誉；（4）对垄断性较强的商品，应提出较多品种，要求对方一一报价，以防对方趁机抬价。询盘也有时由卖方交出，卖方询盘是卖方向买方发出的征询其购买意见的函电。卖方对国外客户发出询盘大多是在市场处于动荡变化及供求关系反常的情况下，目的是探听市场虚实、选择成交时机，主动寻找有利的交易条件。

询盘不是每笔交易必经的程序，如交易双方彼此都了解情况，不需要向对方探询成交条件或交易的可能性，则不必询盘，可直接向对方发盘。

二、如何撰写规范的询盘信函

规范的询盘信函应满足以下几个条件。

1. 格式正确、统一，拟定合理恰当的主题（主要事由）。所有发给客户的函电应该采用统一的格式。

（1）主题中最好有公司名字等。例如，公司名字是ABC，行业是PLASTIC，这封函电的内容是给一款产品报价，那么主题可以写作：ABC/Plastic/quotation of item A。这样做有一个好处，就是可以方便客户以及本公司以后查找信息，对于来往函电很多的客户，可以免去不必要的麻烦。

（2）正文两端对齐。对于段落很多的函电，正文两端对齐会显得很整洁。

（3）函电上最好写上Mr.或者Mrs.××，职位写"Sales Manager"等。

（4）有公司标识以及详细联系资料。

2. 书面整洁。函电的字体、字号要设置好，对一些需要特别提醒客户注意的地方，可以用大写、加粗、特殊颜色等突出显示。

3. 拼写无误。在每封函电发出之前，都应该检查其全部拼写，确保无误。

4. 准确。准确表达我方观点，尽量避免使用有歧义的单词、短语，尽量避免使用俚语等。

5. 详细。能提供给对方详细的资料，有时候企业提出的问题会让客户觉得企业相关人员很细心，很可靠而且非常专业。

6. 条理清晰。能够让客户对函电内容一目了然。

第二节　询盘的范例讲解
（Sample Letters on Inquiries）

一、一般询盘范例

> Dear Sirs,
>
> We have seen your advertisement in the *Overseas Daily News* concerning the new fabrics now available.

We should be obliged if you would send us your pattern books showing the complete range of these fabrics together with your price list.

Please note that we are an ***importer*** of high quality clothing materials, and have large annual requirements for our ***outlets*** throughtout China.

Yours faithfully,

二、进一步询盘范例

April 21, 2010

Re: New Product Line

Dear Mr. Lee,

We have been very pleased with your tablecloths and are now interested in other product lines that your company ***produces***. Please send us catalogs of your ***beddings***, especially quilts and sheets. We are interested in sets as well as individual quilts without matching sheets and pillowcases.

Please let us knowsome information about the standard bed sizes of ***twin, double, queen and king*** as well as the patterns that have proved most popular. We sell sets for both adults and children and would appreciate information on both.

Our last order is selling very successfully and we will most likely be contacting you again soon to recorder. We ***look forward to*** hearing from you on this new line.

Sincerely,

三、具体的询盘范例

Gentlemen,

We are the manufacturers of BM cars and coaches. Our company is a **subsidiary** of BM Inc. of Houston, Texas. We are seeking an **alternative** supplier of automobile DVD players to equip our cars and coaches. As far as we are aware you do not have a local **distributor** of your products in this country.

A full **specification** of our requirements is given on the attached sheet.

Quantity required: 2,500 sets

Delivery: by 20 April, 2010

Please quote us your best **CIF** Larado price, giving a full specification of your products.

We would need to have samples of the players to test in our laboratories before placing a firm order.

We usually deal with new suppliers on the basis of payment in US dollar by **confirmed irrevocable sight letter of credit**.

If your laboratory tests are satisfactory and you can provide us with a good price and service, we will be happy to place more substantial orders **on a regular basis**.

We look forward to receiving an early reply to this inquiry.

Yours truly,

Enclosed: specification and a technical brochure

四、重要词句

1. importer n. 进口商

e.g. But our country is already a big importer of phosphates and especially potash.

但在磷肥尤其是钾肥方面，已经成为一个进口大国。

2. exporter n. 出口商

e.g. Nigeria is the eighth biggest oil exporter in the world.

尼日利亚是世界上第八大石油输出国。

3. outlet n. 销路;商店,商行

e.g. The shoe manufacturer had several outlets.

那家鞋业制造商有好几家商店。

There is a huge sales outlet for pocket computers.

袖珍计算器有极大的市场。

4. produce n. 产品，农产品　v. 产生，生产，提出

e.g. We produce some kinds of kiosk, You can choose it on your basis.

我们生产不同种类的亭子，您可以根据您的要求来选择。

agricultural produce 农产品

5. bedding n. sheets, covers, etc. that you put on a bed 床上用品

e.g. The beautiful sheet will make good bedding for her.

这漂亮的床单是她顶好的床上用品。

We want to buy Pillows, Bedding, Linen, Table Linens, Christmas Accessories.

我们要采购枕头、床上用品、亚麻布、亚麻桌布、圣诞节配饰。

6. twin, double, queen and king: to refer to the sizes of beds and bedclothes.

Twin: the size of a standard single bed; double: the standard size; queen; larger than the standard size but smaller than king-size; king: extra-large size of bedding 单人、双人、大号和加大号床上用品

7. look forward to v. to expect with pleasure 期望、等待

e.g. We are really looking forward to hearing from you.

我们盼望收到贵方回信。

We are really looking forward to cooperating with you.

我们期待着与贵方合作。

8. subsidiary n. 子公司，附属机构

e.g. The subsidiary is in France but the parent company is in America.

该子公司设在法国，但母公司在美国。

British Tyres is a subsidiary of the British Rubber Company.

英国轮胎公司是英国橡胶公司的子公司。

9. alternative adj. 两者择一的

e.g. The goods will be delivered by alternative company.

货物将由另一家公司运送。

I'm looking for the alternative method to solve a dispute.

我正在寻找另外一种方法来解决争端。

10. distributor n. 销售者，经销商

e.g . The company is the local distributor for Volkswagen spare parts.

该公司是本地经销大众汽车零件的商户。

We hope that you will appoint our company as the sole distributor in Japan.

我们希望您能指定我公司作为贵方在日本的独家经销商。

11. specification n. 规格

e.g. The new medicine is taken according to strict specification.

这种新药是严格按照规定服用的。

The designer drew up his specifications for the new car.

设计者为这种新汽车拟定规格。

12. confirmed irrevocable sight letter of credit 保兑的不可撤销即期信用证

　　irrevocable adj. 不能取消的，不能撤回的

e.g. It is an irrevocable letter of credit which can not be altered.

这是一份不可撤销信用证，是不能更改的。

Please open an irrevocable confirmed L/C at sight.

请开立一张不可撤销的即期保兑信用证。

13. CIF到岸价格

到岸价格指由卖方承担货物运抵目的港起卸前的货物成本、运费、保险费和其他劳务费等在内的有关费用的交货价格。

FOB 离岸价格

离岸价格，是指由卖方负责将产品运至买方指定的运输工具上，货物在装运港越过船舷前的有关费用由卖方承担，越过船舷后的有关运费、保险费等由买方承担。

14. on a regular basis 经常性的

e.g. You can get a 5% discount if you order on a regular basis.

如果你方定期给我方下定单，你方即可得到5%的折扣。

15. enclose 随信附上

e.g. I enclose a check for 50 U.S. dollars.

我随信附上一张50美元的支票。

第三节　询盘的实用例句
（Useful Sentences on Inquiring）

以下是一些非常实用的与询盘有关的例句。

1. May I have an idea of your prices?

我可以了解一下你们的价格吗？

2. Please let us know your lowest possible prices for the relevant goods.

请告知你们有关商品的最低价。

3. If your prices are favorable, I can place the order right away.

如果你们的价格优惠，我们可以马上订货。

4. Mr. Li, can you please advise when I get your quotation in CIF term?

李先生，什么时候能得到你们到岸价的实盘？

5. We'd rather have you quote us FOB prices.

我们希望你们报离岸价格。

6. Will you please tell the quantity you require so as enabling us to sort out the offers?

为了便于我方报价，可以告诉我们你们所要的数量吗？

7. We'd like to know what you can offer as well as your sales conditions.

我们想了解你们能供应什么，以及你们的销售条件。

8. How long does it usually take you to make delivery?

你们通常要多久才能交货？

9. Could you make prompt delivery?

你们可以即期交货吗？

10. Would you accept delivery separately over a period of time?

不知你们能不能接受在一段时间里分批交货？

11. Will you please tell us the earliest possible date you can make shipment?

你能否告知我们最早船期？

12. Do you take special orders?

你们接受特殊订货吗？

13. Could you please send us a catalog of your rubber boots together with terms of payment?

你能给我们寄来一份胶靴的目录，连同告诉我们付款方式吗？

14. Heavy enquiries witness the quality of our products.

大量询盘证明我们产品质量过硬。

15. Enquiries for carpets are getting more numerous.

对地毯的询盘日益增加。

16. Enquiries are so large that we can only then allot you 200 cases.

询盘如此之多，我们只能分给你们200箱货。

17. Enquiries are dwindling.

询盘正在减少。

18. Mr. Baker came to Beijing to make an inquiry to China National Textiles Corporation.

贝克先生来北京向中国纺织公司进行询价。

19. In the import and export business, we often make inquiries to foreign suppliers.

在进出口交易中，我们常向外商询价。

20. Your enquiry is too vague to enable us to reply you.

你们的询盘不明确，我们无法答复。

练习题

1. 选择最恰当的答案填空

（1）We certainly accept your offer _____ you will ship the goods during August.

　　A. except　　B. provided　　C. unless　　D. but

（2）_____ you make a 10% reduction, we will have to decline your offer this time.

　　A. When　　B. Except　　C. As　　D. Unless

（3）As we are one of the leading importers in this line, we are _____ a position to handle large quantities.

　　A. at　　B. in　　C. on　　D. of

（4）Please let us have details of your machine tools, _____ your earliest delivery.

　　A. giving us　　B. give us　　C. to give us　　D. given us

（5）We hope to receive your quotation with details _____ the possible time of shipment.

　　A. to include　　B. to be included　　C. including　　D. being included

（6）If you can supply your goods immediately, we shall _____ to place a prompt trial order.

　　A. be prepared　　B. be preparing　　C. prepare　　D. preparing

（7）As we have an extensive business connection in this field, we hope _____ your special terms.

　　A. to give　　B. giving　　C. to be given　　D. to be giving

（8）If your prices are competitive, we are confident _____ the goods in great quantities in this market.

    A. to sell   B. to be selling   C. in being sold   D. in selling

（9）We confirm our fax just dispatched _____ the following items.

    A. offering you firm   B. firm offering you

    C. to be offered you firm   D. to firm offer you

（10）This offer is _____ your acceptance by E-mail on or before October 11.

    A. effective to   B. effectively for

    C. effective for   D. effectively to

2. 将下列语句译成英文

（1）很遗憾，你们所询的商品现在无货。

（2）我们现在无力顾及你方的询盘。

（3）他们答应将以后的询盘转给中国公司。

（4）我们向张经理询问了茶叶的品种、质量和价格等问题。

（5）顾客询问了品种、花色和价格等情况。

（6）一旦价格回升，询盘将恢复活跃。

（7）为了对我们的橙子询价，那家日本公司的一名代表访问了我们。

（8）既然我们已经对你们的产品询价，可否尽快给予答复？

（9）中国丝绸公司收到了英国一家公司的询价单。

（10）能否告知你们将采用哪种付款方式？

3. 将下列词组翻译成中文

（1）regular supply

（2）trade regulation

（3）state-operated

（4）special discount

（5）on the high side

（6）keen competition

（7）under separate cover

（8）packing list

（9）by request

（10）fair average quality

4. 根据下面的内容组织一封询盘函

（1）本公司经营儿童玩具，得知贵公司的儿童玩具特别畅销，尤其是音乐玩具。

（2）询价，尤其是填充玩具和幼儿玩具。

（3）欲与贵公司保持长期合作关系。

第四章　报盘和还盘

Offers and Counter Offers

本章内容提要

本章内容包括如何向客户报盘和对报盘进行还盘。

本章知识重点

如何报盘、就替代品进行报价、对主要交易条件讨价还价，注意掌握术语和一些特殊表达。

第一节 报盘和还盘的写作要点
(How to Write an Offer and a Counter Offer)

一、报盘和还盘

报盘通常是卖方向买方提出某种交易条件（包括商品名称、数量、规格、价格和交货期等），并愿按此条件成交。报盘有实盘（Firm Offer）和虚盘（Non-firm Offer）两种形式。实盘是报盘人在规定的一定期限内，愿意按照所有条件达成交易的肯定表示，实盘一旦被接受，报盘人就不能撤回。虚盘是报盘人所作的非承诺性表示，为无约束力的报盘。一般情况下，多数报盘均为虚盘。虚盘不规定报盘的有效日期，并且附有保留条件，如：The offer is subject to our final confirmation/prior sale.（该报盘以我方最后确认为准/是否提前售出为准）

受盘人收到报盘后，一般需要做出一定的表示。如果不同意或不完全同意对方报盘所提的条件并提出修改条件，即称为还盘。

二、如何撰写规范的报盘

出口商可以直接向客户报盘，也可以在收到客户的询盘后报盘，前者要考虑报盘的准确性和吸引力，后者要注重针对性。但无论如何，其内容都必须准确无误，语气则需诚恳、委婉，并且有说服力，以赢得客户信任，最终取得订单。一般而言，报盘函由以下基本内容组成。

1. 对客户的询盘表示感谢。例如：

We are pleased to receive your E-mail of（date）.

2. 明确答复对方在来信中所询问的事项，准确阐明各项交易条件（如品名、规格、价格、数量、包装、付款方式、装运和保险等），以供对方考虑。例如，

Delivery is to be made within 10 days after receipt of order.

3. 声明此项报盘的有效期及其他约束条件和事项。例如，

This offer is valid for 10 days.

4. 鼓励对方尽早订货，并保证供货令对方满意。例如，

As we have been receiving a rush of orders now, we would advise you to place your order as soon as possible.

三、出口方如何对进口方的还盘进行回复

价格是进出口双方都极为关注的交易条件之一。在出口方报盘后，进口方往往会对价格进行还盘。这时候出口方通常面临三种选择：一是完全接受对方的还价，交易告成；二是坚持原则，拒绝对方的还价；三是针对对方的报价进行再还价，或者是有条件地接受对方的报价。虽然这三种情形在具体语言运用上有所不同，但一般均需包括如下内容。

1. 确认对方的来函

还盘函是一封回信，因此在信的开头应礼节性地感谢对方的来函，并且简洁地表明我方对来函的总体态度。例如，

We are glad to receive your letter of June 1st but sorry to learn that your customers find our quotation too high.

2. 强调价格的合理性，并列明理由

无论最后是否接受对方的报价，我们一般都会先坚持原报价的合理性，同时给出各种适当的理由，或认为报价符合市价，或强调产品的品质超群，或言明利润已降至极限，或指出目前原料价格上涨、人工成本提升等。例如，

As business has been done extensively in your market at this price, we regret to say we can't make further concession.

3. 提出我方条件，并催促对方行动

这部分的写法非常灵活，并没有什么定式而言，关键是要具有说服力，促使对方有所行动。例如，

In order to assist to compete with other dealers in the market, we have decided to reduce 2% of the price quoted to you previously, if your order reaches 500 sets at on time.

第二节　报实盘和还盘的范例讲解
（Sample Letters on Firm Offer and Counter Offer）

一、确认传真报盘范例

Dear Sirs,

In reply to your fax of June 3 which asked us to make an offer on our Blanket No.33, we wish to confirm our fax dispatched on June 6 offering without engagement the following:

Quality: 72 × 84 in.
Weight: 4lbs.
Color: yellow
Quantity: 500 pcs
Price: at USD 40 each piece CIF Montreal
Shipment: During July-August
Terms: Draft at 60 days under an irrevocable L/C

You are *cordially* invited to *take advantage of* this attractive offer which may not be repeated. We are expecting a large order from the United States, and that will cause a sharp rise in price.

As you will have realized from the catalogue we sent you in May, our blanket is a *perfect combination of durability, warmth, softness, and easy care*. We are confident you can do some profitable business.

We look forward to a prompt reply by E-mail, if possible.

Sincerely,

二、报实盘范例

Gentlemen,

Re: Bitter Apricot Kernels, 2010 Crop

We *acknowledge* receipt of your letter dated July 25, from which we note that you wish to have an offer from us for 50 metric tons of the *captioned* goods, for shipment to *Odense*.

In reply, we are making you, *subject to* your reply reaching us by August 15, the following offer:

"50 metric tons of Bitter Apricot Kernels, FAQ2010 crop, at RMB2, 500 per metric ton CIF 2% Odense, shipment per steamer during August/September with transshipment at Copenhagen. Other terms and conditions are the same as usual, with the exception of insurance which will cover ALL Risks and War Risk for 110% of the total invoice value."

As no direct steamer is available from here to Odense, the parcel will have to be transshipped at Copenhagen. Please note that additional cost from Copenhagen to Odense is included in the quoted price.

We look forward to your reply early.

Yours very truly,

三、还盘范例

Dear Sirs,

We thank you for your fax offer of June 1 for 25,000 yards of rayon/woolen mixed fabric and 23,000 yards of dyed cotton shirting.

We immediately contacted our customers and they showed a great interest because there is a growing demand for cotton *textiles*. The prices you quoted, however, are found too much on the high side. ABC Company, one of our customers, *bolds* us that they would possibly take up your entire stock of dyed cotton shirting, provided that the material is offered lower than 35p a yard. ABC is one of the leading *garment* manufacturers in our country, so there is a good chance of *finalizing* an order with them if the present price can be lowered to meet their requirement. We hope you will take advantage of this chance so that you will benefit from the expanding market.

As for the rayon/woolen mixed fabric, our customers hold a fairly large stock at present because of large shipments recently received from Hong Kong. You will, however, receive orders from us soon because we are sure the recent brisk demand will deplete our stock before long.

Under these circumstances, we are most anxious that you will do your utmost to reduce the price for dyed cotton shirting and we await your reply with great interest.

Sincerely,

四、重要词句

1. cordially adv. 诚恳地，诚挚地

e.g. You are cordially invited to the opening ceremony.

诚挚地邀请您参加开业庆典。

As we are opening our first Chinese appliance superstores in Shanghai, we cordially invite high caliber people to join our young and dynamic team.

公司在中国上海的首家大型电器专卖商场已经成功开业，由于业务发展的需要，现诚聘专业人士加盟共谋发展。

2. take advantage of 利用

e.g. So I need to take advantage of that.

所以我需要充分利用这个优势。

A primary requirement for success in the industry is to take advantage of the benefits of new technology and create an infrastructure that affords super efficiency.

要想在行业中获得成功的首要条件就是要利用新技术的优势，建立牢靠的基础，这样才能获得超速效率。

3. perfect adj. 完美的

e.g. Perfect combination of durability, warmth, softness, and easy care.

耐用、暖和、柔软和易于打理的完美结合。

To provide the customers with best products and perfect service is our permanent promise.

为客户提供最好的产品和周到的服务是我们永远的承诺。

It is very important to set up and perfect the inspiration restraint mechanism and competition cooperation mechanism in human resources development.

在企业人才资源开发工作中，建立和完善激励约束机制和竞争合作机制是十分必要的。

4. acknowledge v. 告知收到；承认

e.g. We must acknowledge receipt of his letter.

我们必须向他表明已收到了他的来信。

I hereby acknowledge possession and retention of a copy of this Agreement.

我本人特此承认已拥有和保存本合约副本一份。

5. captioned adj. 标题所说的

e.g. This is to acknowledge receipt of your letter regarding the above-captioned matter.

确认收到您关于提及上述事件的来函。

Subjected my repeated calculations by our company, the captioned price is the lowest.

经我公司反复核算，此价格已是最低价格。

6. Odense n. 奥登赛（丹麦北部城市）

7. subject to 使服从，使遭受

e.g. Yes, we do. This service will be subject to your request.

是的，我们会的。这项服务将根据你们的需要和要求而定。

The dates are rough estimates and are subject to change at any time.

此日期只是粗略估计而已，而且是可以随时变更的。

8. textile n. 纺织品

e.g. We also produce fishing clothes, fishing tents, sleep bags and other textile-made fishing products.

我们还制作捕鱼服、钓鱼帐篷、睡袋及其他纺织品制造的渔业产品。

Their main exports are textiles, especially silk and cotton.

他们的主要出口产品是纺织品，特别是丝绸和棉布。

9. bold v. 大胆地告知

e.g. They bold that they have become the largest company in the city.

他们大胆地宣称他们成为了这个城市规模最大的公司。

10. garment n. 服装

e.g. We are a manufacturer and exporter of garment in northwest China.

我们是中国西北地区的一家服装制造商和出口商。

We have fit style#805 today and noticed significant necklace in the garment.

我们今天配805号样式并注意到服装上显眼的项链。

11. finalize v. 终结，完结

e.g. We so appreciate that you finalize the transaction with us.

感谢贵公司与我方签订这次交易协议。

Urgently confirm the following order in your proforma invoice for shipment to the port of Cotonou / Benin to enable us finalize other matters.

请立即确认形式发票中的下述订单信息，货物运至贝宁科托努港，以便我可以处理其他事情。

第三节　报盘的实用例句
(Useful Sentences on Offering)

以下是一些非常实用的与报盘相关的例句。

1. I come to hear about your offer for fertilizers.

我想知道你们有关化肥的报盘。

2. Please make us an offer by E-mail.

请发邮件报盘。

3. Please make an offer for the bamboo shoots of the quality as that in the last contract.

请把上次合同中订的那种质量的竹笋向我们报个价。

4. We are in a position to offer tea from stock.

我们现在可以供应茶叶现货。

5. We'll try our best to get a bid from the buyers.

我们一定尽力获得买主的递价。

6. I'm waiting for your offer.

我正在等您的报价。

7. We can offer you a quotation based upon the international market.

我们可以按国际市场价格给您报价。

8. We have accepted your firm offer.

我们已接受了你们所报的实盘。

9. We offer firm for reply reaching us 11 a.m. tomorrow.

我们报实盘，以明天上午11点复到为有效。

10. We'll let you have our firm offer next Sunday.

下星期天我们就向你们报实盘。

11. We're willing to make you a firm offer at this price.

我们愿意以此价格为你报实盘。

12. Could you offer us FOB. prices instead of CFR prices?

能向我们报离岸价格而不是成本加运费价吗?

13. All your prices are on CIF. basis.

你们所有价格都是成本加运费、保险费价格。

14. Can you make an offer, CFR London, at your earliest convenience?

您能尽快报一个伦敦港成本加运费价格吗?

15. I'd like to have your lowest quotations, CIF vancouver.

请报温哥华到岸价的最低价格。

16. Please make us an E-mail offer for 5 metric tons of walnut.

请电邮报5公吨核桃仁的价格。

17. Our offer is HKD300 per set of tape-recorder, FOB Tianjin.

我们的报价是每台收录机300元港币，天津离岸价。

18. We quote this article at $250 per M/T CFR Hamburg.

我们报目的港汉堡、每公吨250美元的CFR价。

19. I think the price we offered you last week is the best one.

相信我们上周给你的报价是最好的。

20. No other buyers have bid higher than this price.

没有别的买主的出价高于此价。

21. It was a higher price than the other suppliers offered to us.

此价格比其他供货商给我们的出价要高。

22. We can't accept your offer unless the price is reduced by 5%.

除非你们减价5%，否则我们无法接受你们的报盘。

23. I appreciate your counter offer but find it too low.

谢谢您的还价，可我觉得太低了。

24. I'll respond to your counter offer by reducing our price by three dollars.

我回应你们的还价，减价3美元。

25. I'm afraid the offer is unacceptable.

恐怕你方的报价不能接受。

26. It is difficult to quote without full details.

未说明详尽细节难以报价。

27. Buyers do not welcome offers made at wide intervals.

买主不欢迎报盘间隔太久。

28. We cannot make any headway with your offer.

你们的报盘未得任何进展。

29. Please renew your offer for two days further.

请将报盘延期两天。

30. We regret we have to decline your offer.

很抱歉，我们不得不拒绝你方报盘。

练习题

1. 用合适的介词填空

（1）We shall be glad to receive an offer _____ you _____ bicycles.

（2）Black tea, first grade, is out _____ stock now.

（3）We have _____ present only 50 tons Bitter Apricot Kernels _____ stock.

（4）We will make contact _____ the end-users here and see if they are interested _____ the goods you offered.

（5）You may avail yourselves _____ the opportunity _____ this market if you cable us your acceptance.

（6）If your commodity meets the requirements _____ our market, we feel sure _____ placing a trial order with you.

（7）_____ reply _____ your letter _____ March 20, we are making you, without engagement, the following offer.

（8）_____ separate cover, we have already sent you samples _____ various sizes of shoes.

（9）The buyers made a bid _____ $2,000 per ton _____ walnut-meat.

（10）We are in receipt of your L/C No. 2345 _____ which we thank you very much.

2. 改正下列语句中的错误

（1）In reply, we have the pleasure in informing you that an L/C has been opened in your favor at $2,000.

（2）In international market crude oil is customarily priced at US dollar.

（3）Please do not hesitate to come to us whenever you are for need of our assistance.

（4）We are anxious about receiving your positive reply.

（5）We are in receipt of your letter dated March 10, in which we are pleased to note that you are considering your request.

（6）Only by reducing the price by 5% we can come to business.

（7）Business will still be difficult unless your price will prove to be attractive in the future.

（8）It is always a pleasure to help you whenever we can. But to make a 10% reduction is out of question.

（9）The gap in price is too wide that it can't be bridged over.

（10）Our client said, if you could stretch a point, he would place an additional order of 50 tons.

3. 将下列语句译成英文

（1）我们已经为贵公司预备好报盘了。

（2）下星期就给您正式报盘。

（3）我的报价以合理利润为依据，不会漫天要价。

（4）我们最近的报价大多数都在100美元以下。

（5）现在我们希望你们能以还盘的形式对我方报盘予以答复。

（6）请按同样条件重新报盘。

（7）你的价格太高，买方没有兴趣还盘。

（8）再说，这已经把价格压到生产费用的边缘了。

（9）尽管本公司无法满足你方的特殊要求，但我方仍寄送另一份报价单给你方。

（10）如果你方认为这一报盘可以接受，请即来电，以便我方确认。

4. 将以下内容组合成一封报盘信函

敬启者：

敬请尽早按下列条件来报出商品最低价：

商品：锡箔

数量：50长吨（每长吨2.240磅）

价格：成本加运费到上海，包括宜于出口的包装费用

付款：接受订单后十天开立以你方为收益人的不可撤销的信用证

交货期：2010年6月

早复为盼。

第五章　回复报盘

Reply on Offers

本章内容提要

本章内容包括如何回复报盘，包括接受和婉拒。

本章知识重点

如何对客户提出的报盘表示接受或婉拒，注意语气的把握和常用句式。

第一节　回复报盘的写作要点
（Introduction on How to Reply an Offer）

回复报盘是对对方所报的价格、数量、运货方式等进行回复，包括接受和婉拒。接受表示完全同意交易一方报盘、递盘或还盘的全部内容。报盘、递盘、还盘一经接受，交易即告成立，双方分别履行其所承担的义务。接受应是无条件的，有条件的接受相当于还盘。接受一经发出，不能任意撤销。婉拒是对对方的报盘不满意，或是找到了更合适的贸易伙伴，此时一定要注意措辞。

表示接受的方式有以下两种，内容可繁可简。

1. 接受可简单地用函电表示；有时为了慎重、避免差错和误解，可将双方磋商的主要条件重述一遍，繁简需视情况而定。

2. 在接受的基础上，根据双方达成的协议制好合同、销售确认书或购货确认书寄给对方会签。

第二节　接受和拒绝报盘的范例讲解
（Sample Letters on Accepting and Declining Offers）

一、接受报盘范例

Dear Mr. Smith,

Re: Leather Bags for Men

We accept your counter offer of March 8 and are pleased to confirm having concluded the transaction of the captioned goods with you. Our factory has informed us that they can, at present, *entertain orders* of 30,000 per week. Thus you may rest assured that your order of 50,000 for shipment next month will be fulfilled as contracted.

However, we'd like to emphasize that your L/C must reach here by the end of this month. Otherwise, shipment has to be delayed.

We enclose with this letter our *Sales Confirmation* No. 03M15 *in duplicate*. Please *countersign* and return us one copy for records.

We appreciate your cooperation and trust that our products will turn out to your satisfaction.

Sincerely yours,

二、拒绝报盘范例

Dear Mr. White,

Very Appreciated with your reply to my inquiring on February 19, to quote for the supply of a quantity of strawboards and to send us a sample.

We carefully considered your proposal. We appreciate the good quality of your products, but your prices are much higher than those we have previously paid for strawboards of the same quality. Regretfully, we have decided to place the order elsewhere.

Thank you for your kind help in this matter. We shall continue to place orders and will invite your quotations on this line in the future.

With all good wishes,

Sincerely,

三、还盘范例

Dear Mr. Malcolm,

Thank you for your requirement on asking us to revise our payment terms of our offer.

We appreciate your interest in doing business with us. It will be our honor as well.

For *initial orders* from new customers, the payment term is irrevocable letter of credit or *banker's draft* on or before delivery by our policy, So I am afraid we can't accept the payment terms required by you. But after the first order was processed, we will promise to open an account with 31 days credit term for your future orders.

If you have any question, please feel tree to contact me. My fax number is shown at the bottom of the page. I look forward to cooperating with you.

Sincerely,

四、重要词句

1. entertain orders 接受订货

e.g. At present we can't entertain any fresh orders for Tianyi Brand Men's Shirts.

目前我们不能接受天逸牌男式衬衫的任何新订单。

We are too heavily committed to be able to entertain fresh orders.

我们由于承约过多，目前无法承接新的订单。

2. sales confirmation 销售确认书

（sales-confirmation, confirmation of sales）

e.g. Please be kindly noted that the prices offered in our sales confirmation include 5% of commission.

请注意，我方销售确认书中的价格包括5%的佣金。

The buyer is requested to sign and return one copy of this Sales Confirmation immediately after receipt of the same.

买方应当在收到销售确认书之后立即签章并将其中一份寄回卖方。

3. duplicate n. 副本，复制品

e.g. They are both in duplicate.

它们都是一式两份。

We accept your order and are enclosing you our sales confirmation No, 325 in duplicate of which please countersign and return one copy to us for file.

我们收到贵方定单并随函寄上325号销售确认书一式两份，望签署后寄回一份以便我方存档。

4. countersign v. 会签

e.g. You must countersign on this line of the contract.

你必须在合同的这一行会签。

You will receive our S/C and please countersign and return one copy to us for file.

您将会收到我们的销货合同，并请会签后将一份复印件寄回供我方存档。

5. initial orders 起始订单

e.g. Initial orders will be limited to a minimum of one million units with appropriate financing.

在合适的资金支持下，初始订单会被限制在最少一百万部。

6. banker's draft 银行汇票

e.g. I arranged for some money to be sent from London to Madrid by banker's draft.

我安排用银行汇票的形式将一些钱从伦敦寄到马德里。

7. ...on which you charge your subsequence orders.

后续订单可记账。

第三节　回复报盘的实用例句
（Useful Sentences on a Reply to Offer）

以下是一些非常实用的关于回复报盘的例句。

1. Regretfully, we have decided to place the order elsewhere.

很遗憾，我们决定从别处订货。

2. We are so regretted that, we have decided to accept the other company's offer after comparation.

在综合考虑了利弊之后，我们已决定接受另一家公司的报价。

3. Thank you for your kind help in this matter. We shall be continuing to place orders and will continue to invite your quotations on this line in the future.

此事烦劳贵方，谨表谢忱。我们将继续订购此类商品，并且以后会继续邀请贵方报价。

4. The primary reason for this decision is not the quality but the price.

做出这个决定的主要原因是价格而不是质量。

5. While appreciating the quality of your bicycles, we find your prices are too high to be acceptable.

我们虽赞赏你们自行车的质量，但价格略高难以接受。

6. However, the fact is that your prices appear to be too high to leave us with a small margin of profit.

但事实是，贵方的报价显得过高以至于我们的利润将微薄。

7. To accept your present quotation would mean no profit to us, even the cost.

接受贵方现在的报价就意味着我们将严重亏损，更不要说利润了。

8. Should you be prepared to reduce your price by 5%, we might come to terms.

如果贵方准备降价5%，则我们可以达成一致。

9. It is very appreciated that you would seriously take this matter into

consideration and let us have your reply soon.

希望你们认真考虑此事，并及早答复我们。

10. We thank you for your acceptance of our offer of January 10.

谢谢贵方接受我方1月10日的报价。

11. We accept your counter offer of March 5 and are pleased to confirm having concluded the transaction of the captioned goods with you.

我们接受贵方3月5日的还盘，很高兴与贵方就标题所列商品达成交易。

12. You may begin the manufacturing now as there are only 2 months left before the delivery date stipulated in the S/C.

现在距销售确认书规定的交货日期只有两个月，你们可以开始生产了。

13. We'd like to emphasize that your L/C must reach here by the end of this month. Otherwise, shipment has to be delayed.

我们想强调，贵方信用证必须在本月底前开到我处，否则装运将不得不延期。

14. We enclose with this letter our Sales Confirmation No. 01M12 in duplicate. Please countersign and return us one copy for records.

随函附上我方01M12号销售确认书一式两份，请会签后寄给我方一份存档。

15. If this order is executed satisfactorily, we shall be happy to place further orders with you.

如此次订单的执行令人满意，我们很乐意继续向贵方订货。

练习题

1. 用合适的介词填空

（1）I am sorry to learn _____ your letter of May 4 that you find our prices too high.（of /from）

（2）They have been proved workable _____ the many orders received.（on/by）

（3）Therefore I am afraid we can't accept your payment terms _____ the present time.（on/at）

（4）We hope there will be opportunities for us to work together _____ the future. （in/at）

（5）We would very much like to place further orders with you if you could bring _____ your prices at least by 10%. （up/down）

（6）You may start the manufacturing now as there are only 2 months _____ the delivery date stipulated in the S/C （before/after）

（7）Should you be prepared to reduce your price by 5%, we might come _____ terms. （in/to）

（8）We do our best to keep prices as low as possible _____ sacrificing quality. （with/without）

（9）But hearing in mind the special character of your trade, we have decided to offer you a special discount of 4% _____ a first order for 2,000 pieces. （for/on）

（10）Silence or inactivity _____ the validity of the offer amounts to a declining. （during/among）

2. 将下列语句译成中文

（1）The market at our end has become pretty competitive. In order to sell successfully there, your goods will have to be competitive in price as well.

（2）We have the pleasure of placing an order with you for 1,200 dozen blouses at USD 350 per dozen CIF New York, based on your catalogue No. 67 of June 12.

（3）Should your price be found competitive and delivery date acceptable, we intend to place a large order with you.

（4）We are glad to inform you that we agree to cash payment for your trial order after its delivery at the destination.

（5）Enclosed please find our Sales Confirmation No. 58 in duplicate, one copy of which please sign and return to us for file.

3. 将下列语句译成英文

（1）在综合考虑了利弊之后，我们已决定接受另一家公司的报价。

（2）很遗憾，我们无法接受贵方的付款条件。

（3）我们虽赞赏你们衬衫的质量，但价格略高难以接受。

（4）谢谢贵方接受我方1月21日的报价。

（5）我们接受对方3月8日的还盘，很高兴与贵方就标题所列商品达成交易。

（6）考虑到贵公司业务的特殊之处，对于贵方第一批2 000件订货，我们决定
给予4%的折扣。

（7）我们这样做是因为我们希望在可能的情况下与你们合作，不过我要强调，
这是我们给贵方的最大让步。

（8）贵方价格过高，与现行市场行情有出入。

（9）我们想强调，贵方信用证必须在本月底前开到我处。

（10）我们在发盘时已考虑到长期合作的关系。

4. 将下列内容组合成一封回复还盘的信函

（1）贵方5月5日的传真及棉内衣样品已收到。

（2）我方对样品满意，但是你方报价偏高。

（3）希望贵公司给予优惠。

（4）我方需求量很大，如能合作将继续扩大订货。

第六章　订单及执行

Orders and Their Fulfillment

本章内容提要

本章内容包括如何下订单、续订货，以及如何就执行订单过程中出现的问题进行沟通。

本章知识重点

如何写订货信、续订货信、订单确认书，掌握有关订单的常用表达。

第一节 订单的写作要点
（Introduction on Order）

一、订单的内容和特点

订单是为了要求供应具体数量的货物而提出的一种要求。它是对报盘或询盘后发出报价而促成的结果。订单可以用信函或定制好的订单、传真或E-mail来发送。卖方则用印制好的销售确认书来回复。订单有两种形式：一种是订购信函，另一种是印好的标准订单。

订单的主要特点是正确和清楚。订单或订购信函应包含以下内容。

1.详细的说明、价格、数量以及货号等。

2.说明包装方式、目的港以及装运期。

3.确认在初期洽谈时所同意的付款条件。

4.写明订单号码、日期，负责人签名。

有时因买方所要求的货物无货可供或价格和规格已经改变，卖方不能接受买方的订单。在这种情况下，拒绝接受订单的信函必须非常仔细地撰写，而且要为友谊和今后交易留有余地。此类信函最好介绍一些合适的替代货品，提出还盘和劝说买方接受。

按照相关规定，买方的订单是对欲购货物的出价，在卖方接受以前，不受法律约束。但一旦卖方接受以后，双方就要履行协议，并受法律约束。

二、订单的确认方法和技巧

卖方收到订单后必须进行确认，有的用印制好的销售合同或销售确认书回复。撰写订货确认信函时，应注意以下方法和技巧。

1. 开头应感谢对方的订货，如果决定接受的话，还应在第一段就把这个好消息告诉对方，因为这是对方急切等待的。

2.内容要准确无误，对订货数量、交货日期、货款金额等重要数据进行确认。

3. 如果对方所订货物短缺的话，卖方应马上回函说明原因，使用"high popularity, great demand"等词语解释有利于促销。

4. 如果不能按对方的时间要求交货，应告诉对方可能的交货日期，并强调公司为尽早交货所做的努力。

5. 如果无对方要求的货而有类似的货，可提议以之代替，但最好避免使用"substitute"这个词，因为人们总觉得"substitute"会使被替代的货物不那么令人满意。

6. 如果对方的订购信中有什么不妥或遗漏之处，不应指责对方，只能在感谢对方之后，有策略地请对方说明。

7. 如果不满意买方所列条件，怀疑买方信用，或无现货供应等原因，卖方不能接受买方订单，也要回函说明原因。写谢绝订单的信函时要特别注意语气，不可使友好关系和未来生意受到影响。

8. 订货确认信要充满热情，对对方的惠顾表示真诚的谢意，并趁对方兴致正浓时积极促销，以提高产品销量。

第二节 下订单的范例讲解
（Sample Letters on Placing Orders）

一、下订单范例

Dear Sirs,

Thank you for your letter of 12th July sending us *patterns of cotton prints*. We find both quality and prices satisfactory and are pleased to give you an order for the following items on the understanding that they will be supplied from *current stock* at the prices named:

Quantity	Pattern No.	Price(net)
300	72	33p per yard
450	82	38p per yard
300	84	44p per yard

CIF Lagos

We expect to find a good market for these cottons and hope to place further and larger orders with you in the near future.

Our usual payment term is ***cash against documents*** and we hope it will be acceptable to you. Meanwhile should you wish to make inquiries concerning our ***financial standing***, you may refer to our bank:

The National Bank of Nigeria, Lagos

Please send us your confirmation of sales in duplicate.

Yours faithfully,

二、确认收到订单范例

Dear Sirs,

We are pleased to receive your order of 18th July for cotton prints and welcome you as one of our customers.

For goods ordered we require payment to be made by a confirmed and irrevocable letter of credit payable at sight upon presentation of shipping documents. Please let us know immediately whether you agree to our terms. As soon as we receive your reply in the affirmative, we shall confirm supply of the prints at the prices stated in your letter and arrange for ***dispatch*** by the first available steamer upon receipt of your L/C.

When the goods reach you, we feel confident you will be completely satisfied with them at the prices offered as they represent exceptional value.

As you may not be aware of the wide range of goods we deal in, we are enclosing a copy of our catalogue and hope that this first order of yours will lead to further business between us and have a good start for our relationship.

Yours faithfully,

三、订单附信范例

Dear Sirs,

We thank you for your letter of 2nd July and are glad to inform you that your samples are satisfactory. ***Enclosed please find*** our order No.237 for four of the items.

All these items are urgently required by our customers. We, therefore, hope you will make delivery at an early date.

Yours faithfully,

ORDER FORM

September 27, 2010

Qnty	Item	Catalogue No.	CIF Sydney NET
250	Bed Sheets, 106 cm, blue	75	USD 2.50 each
250	Bed Sheets, 120 cm, *primrose*	82	USD 3.00 each
500	pillow cases, blue	117	USD 1.80 each
500	Pillow cases, primrose	121	USD 1.80 each

Packing: In cotton cloth ***bales***

Shipment: Prompt shipment from Shanghai

Payment: By irrevocable L/C available by draft at sight

四、重要词句

1. patterns of cotton prints 棉布印花样式

2. current stock 现货

e.g. We are pleased to place an order for the following items on the understanding that they will be supplied from current stock at the prices mentioned before.

兹订购下列各项产品，谅能按所订价格供应现货。

3. cash against documents 凭单付款

e.g. We regret we can't accept cash against document on the arrival of goods at destination.

很抱歉，我们不能同意用"货抵目的地付款交单"方式付款。

Please inform us whether C.A.D.（cash against documents）is acceptable.

请告知凭单付款的支付方式能否接受。

4. financial standing 财务状况

e.g. ABC company has referred us to your Bank for detailed information about its financial standing and business capacity.

ABC公司介绍我公司向你行了解该公司的财务状况和业务能力等详细情况。

We would highly appreciate it if you could inform us, in confidence, of the financial standing of the said firm.

如果以保密的方式告知我方该公司的财务状况，我们将不胜感激。

5. The National Bank of Nigeria, Lagos位于拉各斯的尼日利亚国民银行

6. For goods ordered we require payment to be made by a confirmed and irrevocable letter of credit payable at sight upon presentation of shipping documents.

对所订之货，我们要求用保兑的不可撤销的信用证，在出示装运单据时凭即期汇票付款。

7. dispatch n. 发货，发送

e.g. We regret for the delay of our dispatch.

对发货延误我们深表歉意。

Can you confirm the dispatch date?

你可以确定发货日期吗?

dispatch order 发运单

dispatch advice 发运通知

8. Qnty/QTY: abbreviation of quantity 数量的缩写

e.g. First, get the order Qnty/QTY right and then you all can do material planning.

首先,把订货数额更正,然后你们才可以做材料计划。

Stock Qnty/ QTY 库存数量

9. Enclosed please find 随信附上

10. primrose 淡黄色

e.g. Which color do you prefer, primrose or blue?

你更喜欢哪种颜色,浅黄还是蓝色?

11. bale 包,捆

e.g. Enclosed please find the invoice for 500 bale cotton, deliver FOR for your account.

兹寄上以贵司为抬头的关于500包棉花的发票一张,请查收。

Would you please send the goods in cotton bales?

请你方将货物用棉布包好发送,可以吗?

第三节　有关订单的实用例句
(Useful Sentences on Orders)

以下是一些非常实用的有关订单的例句。

1. According to our records, it has been a long time that we had no any business between us since the last order processed, and we are wondering whether there is something "happened". 据我公司记载,自上笔交易以来,我们的业务已中断了很长时间,不知是否因为我方服务不周所致,敬请告知。

2. Should you think favorably of our application, kindly hand us your order-sheet. 如蒙惠顾，请寄订单为盼。

3. I have received your price list, and shall be appreciated if you will send me by rail as early as possible as follows. 价格表已收到，请尽可能迅速以铁路货运下列商品，不胜感激。

4. I shall be thankful if you will provide us with fifty tons of coal, in accordance with your sample. 请按照贵公司提供的样品，供应我公司50吨煤炭，谢谢。

5. As the expiry date of the L/C being May 31, please advise your banker to extend the expiry date from May 31 to June 10. 信用证有效期为5月31日，请通知贵方银行将其延长至6月10日。

6. We confirm here with your telegraphic order of the June 10, for 100 cwt. of the best sugar. 贵公司6月10日电报关于高级砂糖100英担的订单已收到，并予以确认。

7. The machines ordered on April 10 were dispatched to your address yesterday. 4月10日所定机器已于昨天运出，请查收。

8. In thanking you for your esteemed order of the May 5, I inform you that it has been executed today. 感谢您5月5日的订单，本日已经履约，特此奉告。

9. We have none of this particular make in stock at the moment. We are afraid we can't guarantee delivery within less than three months after receipt of orders. 目前，关于此类特制品没有存货。因此我们很担心在接到订单后的三个月内不能交货，敬请谅解。

10. To my deep regret, the buyer of these goods has just cancelled the order, a fact which compels me to cancel my order with you. 非常抱歉，兹因购货人已向我公司撤单，迫使我公司只好向贵公司取消这一次订货。

11. We have received your letter of July 7, 2010 together with an order for 1,000 Sewing Machines. Enclosed is our sales confirmation No. 345 in duplicate, one copy of which please sign and return to us for our file. 你公司2010年7月7日来函内附1 000台缝纫机订单已经收到。兹附寄第345号销售确认书一式两份，请会签并寄回一份以便存档。

12. Your order No. 85 for 100,000 yards of Cotton Prints Art. No.1001 has been booked. Please let us know the color assortment at once and open the covering L/C in our favor according to the terms contracted. 我已接受贵方85号订单订货号1001印花布10万码。请告颜色搭配并按合同规定的条款开立以我方为抬头的有关信用证。

13. We learn that an L/C covering the above-mentioned goods will be established immediately. You may rest assured that we will arrange for dispatch by the first available steamer with the least possible delay upon receipt of your L/C. 我方获悉上述货物的有关信用证即将开出。请放心，一收到你方信用证，我方将尽早安排第一艘可以订到舱位的轮船装货。

14. Please note that the stipulations in the revelant credit should fully conform with the terms as stated in our S/C in order to avoid subsequent amendments. 请你方注意，信用证的条款必须与我方销售确认书的条款完全相符，以免日后修改。

15. If this first order is satisfactorily executed, we shall place further orders with you. 如果这第一份订单的执行情况很令人满意的话，我们将会继续订货。

16. It is regrettable to see an order dropped owing to no agreement on price; however, we wish to recommend you another quality at a lower price for your consideration. 很遗憾由于价格谈不拢，只得放弃了一份订单。不过，我们希望向你方推荐另一种价格较低的货物供你方考虑。

17. We trust that you will give this order your prompt and careful attention. 我们相信你方对这份订单会进行快速认真的办理。

18. Please let us know how soon you can dispatch this order. 请告知我方订货何时能发运。

19. Please supply... in accordance with the detail in our order No... 请照我方第……号订单供货。

20. We confirm having purchased from you shirts, for which a confirmation of order enclosed for your reference. 我方确认向你方订购衬衫，随函附上订购确认书一份，供参考。

练习题

1. 用合适的词或词组填空

（1）Thanks for your offer of June 3, but we regret that we can't accept it unless price reduces _____ approximately 7%.

（2）_____ reference to your letter of May 6, we are pleased to give you an order for the following.

（3）Enclosed is our order _____ 300 sets of Transistor Radios T123.

（4）We are _____ receipt of your letter of July 8 and are pleased to give an order for the following.

（5）Please see _____ it that our goods meet our requirements.

（6）_____ receipt of your reply, we will open an L/C by fax.

（7）Please draw _____ us for the invoice amount at the time of shipment.

（8）As _____ as we receive your confirmation, we will arrange shipment.

（9）_____ to a serious shortage of shipping space, we can't deliver these machines until 31.

（10）Because _____ shortage of raw materials, we can't accept any further orders for some time.

2. 选择最佳答案填空

（1）This order _____ the sample you sent us on March 1.

    A. is placed on   B. places on   C. is placed at   D. placed at

（2）We would ask you to do everything possible _____ punctual shipment.

    A. ensurin   B. to be ensured   C. to ensure   D. while ensuring

（3）We hope you give your usual best attention _____ this order.

    A. for carrying out   B. to the execution of

    C. by filling out   D. in the performance of

（4）We must have the goods not later than October 1 _____ our stock is running short.

    A. when   B. that   C. which   D. as

（5）We have accepted your Order No.315. Please open the relevant L/C _____ here two weeks prior to the date shipment.

A. which must reach　　B. when must reach

C. it reaches　　　　　D. that reaches

（6）We have decided to place a trial order for the following goods _____ the terms stated in your letter.

A. with　　B. on　　C. by　　D. at

（7）Please send us as soon as possible the following goods _____ in your current spring catalog.

A. that listed　　B. which listed　　C. to be listed　　D. as listed

（8）We are enclosing our latest catalogue _____ the hope that some of the items may be of interest to you.

A. at　　B. by　　C. in　　D. for

（9）_____ we would like to supply you with product, we are unable to fill your order owing to the heavy backlog of commitments.

A. as much as　　B. much as　　C. very much　　D. as

（10）We must apologize _____ you _____ being unable to fill your present order.

A. to...on　　B. to … as　　C. to … about　　D. to … for

3. 将下列语句译成英文

（1）如蒙贵方就此笔订货立即安排装运，则不胜感激。

（2）收到你方订单已有时日，由于疏忽我方未曾告知你方。

（3）由于你方库存没有所需货品，我们想知道是否有合适的代用品。

（4）我们确认已向你方按下列条件购买3 000打衬衫。

（5）请尽快提供如下产品。

（6）非常遗憾地通知贵公司，因为购货人对贵公司价格500美元不予确认，因此要求您取消此订单。

（7）据我公司记载，自上笔交易以来，我们的业务已中断了很长时间，不知是否因为我方服务不周所致，敬请告知。

（8）4月10日所定机器已于昨天运出，请查收。

（9）如蒙惠顾，请寄订单为盼。

（10）我们确保你方会在各方面对货物感到满意并满足你方需要。

4. 将下列内容组合成一封向卖方下订单的信函

（1）接到对方5月20日对我方体育用品的订货。

（2）确认价格供货并安排下周海路发运。

（3）随函附寄一份产品目录。

（4）希望长期合作。

第七章　购货合同及销售确认书

Purchase Contract and Sales Confirmation

本章内容提要
本章内容包括购货合同及销售确认书。

本章知识重点
了解购货合同和销售确认书的主要内容及格式，掌握有关合同的常用句式。

第一节　合同的写作要点
（Introduction on Contracts）

一、购货合同

合同针对两个或两个以上的人或团体，合同具有法律效力的基本要求是签约的团体或个人应该具有法律能力和签约自由。签约人必须有签约的倾向和目的而且目的必须合乎法律。合同可以分为正式合同和非正式合同两种。

在国际贸易活动中被普遍接受的合同是正式合同。通过多次函电往来，或者经过多轮谈判之后，以交易双方商定的条件为基础，正式签订购货合同。签订购货合同对交易双方都是至关重要的，没有签字的购货合同不能成为有效的法律文件。在合同签字前，卖方应该明确如下几点。

1. 所有与交易有关的条款必须经过充分讨论并接受。

2. 所有的条款必须易懂，合同格式要整洁。

3. 确保没有语言错误。

4. 必须有适当的授权人签字。

正式的购货合同一般包括三部分：约首、约文和约尾。约首通常包括缔约缘由、合法依据、缔约当事人和缔约地点等；约文通常涵盖缔约条款以及对缔约当事人所应该享有的权利与义务的详细阐述；结尾通常包括文字效力、当事人签字、盖印和合同终止等。在撰写合同时要首字母大写来提及合同条款，使用条件从句涵盖合同细节；要注意使用法律条文"必须"来要求法律义务，注意使用"因此"等文字。

二、销售确认书

销售确认书是交易双方在通过磋商达成交易后，由卖方出具并寄给对方加以确认的列明达成交易条件的书面证明，经买卖双方签署的销售确认书是有效的法律文件，对买卖双方具有同等的约束力。在国际贸易中常简写为S/C。

三、合同条款

在拟定合同之前，我们首先应掌握有关合同条款的基础知识。

1. 出口贸易买卖合同的条款

一般来讲，出口贸易买卖合同的所有条款，即合同的标的（货物的品名、品质、数量、包装）、价格与支付条款、交易条件（运输、保险）、预防与解决争议的条款（检验、索赔、不可抗力和仲裁）等，其中品质、数量、包装、装运、价格、支付保险等七项为主要条款或主要交易条件。买卖双方欲达成交易、订立合同时至少必须注明这七项条款（特殊情况可以例外）。至于其他交易条款，特别是检验、索赔、不可抗力和仲裁，它们虽非确立合同不可缺少的条款，但是为了提高合同质量，防止或减少争议的发生以及便于解决可能发生的争议，买卖双方在订立合同时也不能忽视。

2. 品名质量条款

商品的名称和质量是买卖双方首先需要确定的交易条件，也是买卖双方交易的物质基础。因此，商品的名称和质量是进出口合同中的主要条款之一。在进出口交易中表示品质的方法可分为两类：用实物样品和用文字说明表示。用实物样品表示时，合同中应注明凭以达成交易的样品的编号，必要时还要列出寄送样品的日期。在用文字说明表示时，应针对不同交易的具体情况在合同中明确规定商品的名称、规格、等级、标准、品牌、商标或产地等内容。在以说明书或图样表示商品质量时，还应在合同中列明说明书、图样的名称、份数等内容。

3. 数量条款

合同中的数量条款主要包括成交商品的具体数量和计量单位，有的合同还需要规定确定数量的方法。在实际进出口业务中，有些商品可以精确计量，而有些商品受本身特性、生产、运输或包装条件及计量工具的限制，交货时不易精确计算。为了合同的顺利履行，减少争议，买卖双方通常在合同中规定数量的机动幅度条款，允许卖方交货时数量在一定范围内浮动。合同中的数量机动幅度条款一般有溢短装条款和"约"量条款（较少使用）两种。

4. 包装条款

合同中的包装条款一般包括包装材料、包装方式、包装规格、包装标志和包装费用的负担等内容。

例如，用涤纶袋包装，35镑装一袋，6袋装一箱。箱子需用以金属作衬里的木箱，包装费用由卖方承担。

To be packed in poly bags, 35 pounds in a bag, 6 bags in a sealed wooden case which is lined with mental, the cost of packing is for seller's account。

包装条件应在合同中具体、明确约定，对特别精密的仪器设备还必须提出防震条件，有的商品要提出防潮要求，不宜侧置的商品要在包装上注明向上标志等。

5. 装运条款

进出口合同中的装运条款通常包括转运时间、装运港或装运地、目的港或目的地，以及部分装运和转运等内容，有的还规定卖方应予交付的单据和有关转运通知的条款。

例如，2010年5月装运，由上海至纽约。卖方应在装运月份前45天将备妥货物可供装船的时间通知买方，允许部分装运和转运。

Shipment during May from Shanghai to New York. The Sellers advise the Buyers 45 days before the month of shipment of time the goods will be ready for shipment. Partialshipment and transshipment are allowed.

6. 价格条款

国际货物买卖合同中的价格条款一般包括商品的单价和总值两项基本内容，单价通常由计量单位、单位价格、计价货币、贸易术语四部分组成，有时会涉及折扣和佣金。以上四者缺一不可，且前后左右顺序不能随意颠倒。单价总额与总值的金额要吻合，且币别保持一致，如果数量允许增加，则合同中的总额也应相应增减。

例如，每公吨800美元FOB上海减折扣5%。

USD 800 per metric ton FOB Shanghai less 5% discount.

折扣是指卖方按照原价给予买方一定百分比的减让，一般由买方在付款时预先扣除。折扣常见的表示方法有：① 文字表示法，如USD20.00/PC FOB Toronto less 2% discount; ② 缩写表示法，如USD20.00/PC FOB D2%Toronto。

佣金是卖方或买方支付给中间商为其对货物的销售或购买提供中介服务的酬金。佣金包括明佣和暗佣，明佣直接显示在价格上，一般在货款结算时支付给中介商；暗佣是暗地付给中间商，不显示在价格上。明佣常见的表示方法有：① 文字表示法，如USD20.00/PC FOB Toronto including 3% commission；② 缩写表示法，如USD20.00/PC FOB C3%Toronto。

7. 支付条款

在出口贸易中，货款的收付主要涉及所使用的支付工具、支付时间、支付地点和支付方式等问题。买卖合同中支付条款的内容视所采用的收付方式而定。

8. 保险条款

保险条款的内容依选用贸易术语的不同而有所区别：按FOB、FCA、CFR或CPT条件成交，合同中的保险条款只需规定保险由买方办理：按CIF或CIP条件成交的保险条款则需具体规定保险金额、投保险别和保险适用的条款内容。

9. 检验条款

在国际货物买卖合同中商品检验条款的内容主要有检验时间与地点、检验机构和检验证书等。

10. 索赔条款

国际货物买卖合同中的索赔条款有两种规定方法：异议与索赔条款和罚金条款。拟定索赔条款应注意索赔的对象和确定合理的期限。

11. 不可抗力条款

国际货物买卖合同不可抗力条款的内容包括不可抗力事件的范围，对不可抗力事件的处理原则和方法、不可抗力事件发生后通知对方的期限和方法以及出具证明文件的机构等。

四、签约函

进出口业务中，买卖合同一般由我方制作。合同做好后，我方应及时寄给对方让其签署。寄合同时，我方一般要在合同外附上一封简短的书信——签约函。签约函的内容一般包括以下三点。

1. 对成交表示高兴，希望合同顺利进行。

2. 告知对方合同已寄出，希望其予以会签。

3. 催促对方尽早开立信用证。

第二节 合同及销售确认书的范例讲解
(Sample Letters on Contracts and S/C)

一、合同范例

Sample Contract

No. A. S. 102-99

Buyers: *Anderson Trading Company, Denmark*

Sellers: *Guangdong Native Produce Imp. & Exp. Co.*

This contract is made by and between the Buyers and the Sellers, whereby the Buyers agree to buy and the sellers agree to sell the under-mentioned goods according to the terms and conditions stipulated below:

Commodity: *Wuyi Peanuts*

Specifications: *FAQ 2010 Crop*

Quantity: *100 m/t.*

Unit Price: *USD 500.00 per m/t, CIF Aarhus Denmark*

Total value: *USD 50,000.00*

Packing: *In 3-ply gunny sacks of 50 kg each*

Shipping marks:

Insurance: *To be effected by the seller for 100% of invoice value plus 10% against All Risks*

Terms of shipment: *During July, 2010 with transshipment at Copenhagen*

Port of shipment: *Huangpu, China*

Port of destination: *Aarhus, Denmark*

Terms of payment: *By irrevocable L/C payable by draft at sight. The L/C should reach the seller 30 days before the time of shipment and to remain valid for negotiation in China until the 15th day after the day of shipment.*

Done and signed in Guangzhou on this twentieth day of April, 2010.

二、销售确认书范例

SALES CONFIRMATION

合同号：（CONTRACT NO）：

日期（DATE）：

签约地点（SIGNED AT）：

卖方（SELLERS）：

买方（BUYERS）：

传真（FAX）：

地址（ADDRESS）：

兹经买卖双方同意按下列条款成交：

THE UNDERSIGNED SELLERS AND BUYERS HAVE AGREED TO CLOSE THE FOLLOWING TRANSACTIONS ACCORDING TO THE TERMS AND CONDITIONS STIPULATED BELOW：

货号（ART. NO.）：

品名及规格（DESCRIPTION）：

数量（QUANTITY）：

单价（UNIT PRICE）：

金额（AMOUNT）：

总值（TOTAL VALUE）：

1. 数量及总值均有×%的增减，由卖方决定。

WITH×%MORE OR LESS BOTH IN AMOUNT AND QUANTITY ALLOWED AT THE SELLERS OPTION.

2. 包装（PACKING）：

3. 装运唛头（SHIPPING MARK）：

4. 装运期（TIME OF SHIPMENT）：

5. 装运口岸和目的地（LOADING AND DESTINATION）：

6. 保险由卖方按发票全额110%投保至××为止的××险。

INSURANCE：TO BE EFFECTED BY BUYERS FOR 110% OF FULL

INVOICE VALUE COVERING ×× UP TO ×× ONLY.

7. 付款条件（PAYMENT）：买方须于××年××月××日将保兑的、不可撤销的、可转让可分割的即期信用证开到卖方。信用证议付有效期延至上列装运期后15天在中国到期，该信用证中必须注明允许分运及转运。

BY CONFIRMED, IRREVOCABLE, TRANSFERABLE AND DIVISIBLE L/C TO BE AVAILABLE BY SIGHT DRAFT TO REACH THE SELLERS BEFORE ×× AND TO REMAIN VALID FOR NEGOTIATION IN CHINA UNTIL 15 DAYS AFTER THE AFORESAID TIME OF SHIPMENT. THE L/C MUST SPECIFY THAT TRANSIMENT AND PARTIAL SHIPMENTS ARE ALLOWED.

8. 仲裁条款（ARBITRATE CLAUSES）：凡因本合同引起的或与本合同有关的争议，均应提交中国国际经济贸易委员会，按照申请仲裁时该会现行有效的仲裁规则进行仲裁，仲裁地点在××，仲裁裁决是终局性的，对双方均有约束力。

ANY DISPUTE ARISING OUT OF IN CONNECTION WITH THIS CONTRACT SHALL BE REFERRED TO CHINA INTERNATIONAL ECONOMIC AND TRADE ARBITRATION COMMISSION FOR ARBITRATION IN ACCORDANCE WITH ITS EXISTING RULES OF ARBITRATION. THE PLACE OF ARBITRATION SHALL BE××. THE ARBITRAL AWARD IS FINAL AND BINDING UPON THE TWO PARTIES.

备注（REMARK）：

卖方（SELLERS）：　　　　买方（THE BUYERS）：

三、发送订购中国东北大豆的销售确认书范例

Dear David Bush,

Thank you for your order of May 25th for 600,000 M/T of Northeast China's soybeans. We enclose our S/C No. 334 *in duplicate*, of which please *counter-sign* and return one copy to us for our file.

Enclosed please also find our latest illustrated catalogue for other products. If you find them interesting, please let us know. We will send you our best quotations upon receipt of your specific enquiry.

We await your early reply.

Yours faithfully,

四、重要词句

1. in duplicate 一式两份

e.g. Please send the duplicate of the contract countersigned to us.

请将已会签的合同副本寄给我方。

类似的表达有：

in triplicate 一式三份

in quadruplicate 一式四份

in quintuplicate 一式五份

in sextuplicate 一式六份

in septuplicate 一式七份

in octuplicate 一式八份

in nonuplicate 一式九份

in decuplicate 一式十份

2. counter-sign v. 会签

协议、契约、文本等涉及双方（或多方）各执一份时，需要双方（或多方）在所有文本上会签，然后各执一份。

e.g. As requested in your previous fax, we have made out our Sales Confirmation No. 1001 in duplicate and shall appreciate your sending back one copy duly counter-signed.

按贵方上次传真的要求，我方已备好第1001号销售确认书一式两份，并请及时会签后退我方一份。

3. Main clauses in a contract

（1）Commodity

——Name of commodity

——Quantity of commodity

——Quality of commodity

——Packing of commodity

（2）Price

——Unit price: currency unit, unit price figure, measurement unit and delivery terms.

——Total amount

（3）Payment

——Terms of payment

——Date and location of payment

（4）Shipment

—— Time of shipment

—— Port of shipment and port of destination

—— Shipping advice

—— Partial shipment and transshipment

（5）Shipping Marks

（6）Loading and Discharging

（7）Insurance

第三节 订立合同的实用例句
（Useful Sentences for Entering into a Contract）

以下是一些非常实用的关于订立合同的例句。

1. We are pleased to enclose our contract No. 3901 in two copies. If you find everything in order, please sign and return one copy for our file.

我们很高兴附上我方第3901号合同两份。如果你方认为一切妥当，请会签后寄回一份，以便我方存档。

2. We have sent you our Sales Contract No. 22 in duplicate for your confirmation.

我们寄去了第22号销售合同一式两份，以便你方确认。

3. We are glad to have concluded this transaction with you.

我们很高兴与你方达成了这笔交易。

4. The conclusion of the dealing is certainly not the ending. It is only the beginning, and a good one, of the long and friendly business relations between us.

这笔交易的达成当然不是结束。这仅仅是个开端，而且是我们之间建立长期友好业务关系的一个良好开端。

5. Enclosed please find our Sales Contract No. 397 in duplicate for your counter-signature. Please send one copy back to us at your earliest convenience.

随函附上我方第397号销售合同一式两份，请您会签。在您方便的时候，请尽早给我们寄回一份。

6. The contract is provisional, not exists forever.

这个合同是临时的，不是永远有效。

7. As an integral part of the contract, the inspection of goods has its special importance.

作为合同的一个组成部分，商品检验具有特殊的重要性。

8. The firms, when they draw up a contract, specify a procedure for arbitrating any dispute that may arise.

当公司拟定一份合同时，要具体说明解决仲裁纠纷的指定程序。

9. We have duly received your Sales Contract No.666 in duplicate for 100 sets of sofas.

我们如期收到您寄送的关于100套沙发的销售合同一式两份。

10. As requested, we have counter-signed it and now enclose the duplicate for

your file.

按照要求，我们已经会签完毕，现将副本提供给你方存档。

11. They sign an agency agreement or an agency contract.

他们签署了一份代理协议或代理合同。

12. Enclosed please find the draft of the sales confirmation and double-check it against our negotiation results.

随信附上销售确认书的草案，请根据我们的洽谈结果对内容做再次核查。

13. We are so pleased to bring the transaction into conclusion with your company and sending you our purchasing confirmation as attachment.

我们非常高兴与贵公司达成交易，并在此作为附件寄送我们的购货确认书。

14. Enclosed please find a duplicate of our company standard leases and the order of rent payment. Please sign and send them to us so as to return one copy to you after our counter-signature.

随函附送我公司标准租约一式两份，以及租金付款指令。请将两份租约签字后，寄给我公司以便会签后退贵公司一份。

15. Enclosed is a specimen of sales confirmation for your reference.

随函寄来销售确认书样本一份，以供参考。

16. Kindly note that the prices given in our sales confirmation include × × % of commission.

请注意，我方销售确认书中的价格包括××％佣金。

17. The seller shall not be held liable for failure or delay in delivery of the entire lot or a portion of the goods under this sales confirmation in consequence of any force major incidents.

本确认书内所属全部或部分商品，如因人力不可抗拒的原因，以致不能履约或延迟交货，卖方将对此不负责。

18. If we again fail to receive your L/C in time, we shall have to cancel our sales confirmation.

如果贵方的信用证仍然不能及时抵达我方，我们将不得不取消销售确认书。

19. One additional copy/photocopy of invoice and transportation documents to

be presented for L/C issuing bank's file.

一份额外的发票和运输文件的副本或影印件须提交给开证行做为存档之用。

20. We can grant you 5% discount on orders exceeding $1,000 in value/on repeat order.

价值超过1 000美元的订货/再次订货折扣按5%计算。

练习题

1. 将以下内容译成英文

（1）销售确认书　　（2）一式三份　　　　　　（3）发票金额

（4）仲裁条款　　　（5）以卖方为受益人　　　（6）由卖方决定

（7）销售合同　　　（8）以便存档

2. 选择最佳答案填空

（1）An agreement is _____ as a result of the process of offer and acceptance.

　　A. included　　B. reached　　C. had　　D. resulted

（2）The shipped fruits may _____ because of the long journey.

　　A. change　　B. deteriorate　　C. eat　　D. rot

（3）To avoid possible dispute _____ quality, both parties should describe the goods exactly as the Buyer and Seller intend them to be.

　　A. on　　B. in　　C. of　　D. at

（4）The exporter must pack the goods _____ strict conformity _____ the contract stipulations.

　　A. on...on　　B. on...with　　C. in...with　　D. of...of

（5）Improper packing may _____ local customs to either reject the goods or levy a fine.

　　A. make　　B. force　　C. cause　　D. give

（6）The currency to be denominated in the contract is _____ .

　　A. cost term　　　　　　B. interest clause

　　C. cost escalation clause　　D. payment term

（7）_____ is only used in west countries.

    A. Payment term   B. Quoted price

    C. Interest clause   D. Cost escalation clause

（8）As a general rule, export goods are always inspected by the _____ before shipment.

    A. shipper   B. buyer   C. agent   D. distributor

（9）Should any _____ be found after the arrival of the goods at the port of destination, the Buyer would lodge a claim.

    A. differences   B. difficulties   C. discrepancies   D. mistakes

（10）Warranty clause is suitable to certain products such as _____ .

    A. native produce   B. mushrooms   C. canned food   D. machines

3. 将下列语句译成英文

（1）根据近日往来函件，请尽快起草销售合同并邮寄两份给我们会签。

（2）请尽快返还一份以便我方存档。

（3）我方确认向你方订购衬衫，随函附上订购确认书一份，以供参考。

（4）如你方将价格降至我方水平，我们有可能达成交易。

（5）近来我们的电子邮件往来促成了这笔交易。

4. 将销售确认书译成中文

Sales Contract

No. 95GF-202

    Sellers: Shandong Native Product Imp. & Exp. Corp.

    Buyers: The General Trading Company Denmark

    This Contract is made by and between the Buyers and the Sellers, whereby the Buyers agree to buy and the sellers agree to sell the under-mentioned commodity according to the terms and conditions stipulated below:

    Commodity: Bitter Apricot Kernels

    Specifications: FAQ 2010 Crop.

    Quantity: 50 metric tons

Unit Price: at USD 480 per metric ton CIF Odense

Total Value: USD 24, 000（Say US Dollars Twenty-Four Thousand Only）

Packing: In 3-ply gunny bags of 50 kgs. each

Insurance: To be effected by the seller for 100% of the invoice value plus 10% against All Risks and War Risk

Time of shipment: During December, 2010, with transshipment at Copenhagen

Port of shipment: Qingdao, China.

Port of destination: Odense, Denmark

Terms of Payment: By irrevocable letter of credit payable by draft at sight. The L/C should reach the seller 30 days before the time of shipment and to remain valid for negotiation in China until the 15th day after the date of shipment.

Done and signed in Guangzhou on this 15th day of September, 2010.

第八章　支付

Payment

本章内容提要

本章内容涉及支付方式、支付工具、支付条款等。

本章知识重点

如何撰写信函催证、通知开证、要求修改信用证、要求改用其他支付方式以及对变更支付方式的回复，重点掌握与各种支付方式有关的术语和特殊表达。

第一节　支付与信用证的写作要点
（Introduction on Payment and L/C）

一、支付形式

支付是国际贸易中的重要环节之一，其方式由买卖双方商定，主要有如下几种。

1. 预付现金（Cash in advance）。此种支付方式常用于进口商信誉不好，或不为出口商所了解，或进口商所在国的政治、经济不稳定。

2. 开立账户交易（Open an account）。此种支付方式常用于买卖双方已相互信赖。

3. 使用付款交单（D/P）或承兑交单（D/A）。通过银行进行托收。托收按其性质来讲反映的是一种商业信用，卖方能否安全、及时地收回货款取决于买方的信用如何。

4. 开立信用证（L/C）。开立信用证是目前使用最广泛的付款方式，信用证是银行开立的一种有条件的付款保证书。信用证支付的通常做法是：先由买方通知其往来银行开立以卖方为受益人的信用证，再由买方的往来银行（开证行）把信用证寄给其在卖方国家的往来银行，后者通知卖方。

就出口商（卖方）利益而言，开立信用证方式优于付款交单，见票即付交单优于见票后才付款交单，付款交单优于承兑交单。

由于信用证提供的是银行信用，只要出口方提供的单据与信用证规定严格一致，银行就会付款，这一做法使得与陌生进口方的交易更简单，对进出口双方均提供了一定的保护，因此在国际贸易中支付多是通过信用证来进行。

二、开立信用证的步骤

申请开立信用证具体有以下三个步骤。

1. 递交有关合同的副本及附件

进口商在向银行申请开证时，要向银行递交进口合同的副本以及所需附件，如进口许可证、进口配额证、某些部门的审批文件等。

2. 填写开证申请书

进口商填写银行统一规定格式的开证申请书一式三份，一份留业务部门、一份留财务部门、一份交银行。填写开证申请书必须按合同条款的具体规定，写明信用证的各项要求，内容要明确、完整。

3. 缴纳保证金

按照国际贸易的习惯做法，进口商向银行开立信用证，应向银行缴付一定比例的保证金，其金额一般为信用证金额的百分之几到百分之几十，具体比例根据进口商的资信情况而定。在我国的进出口业务中，开证行根据不同企业和交易情况，要求开证申请人缴付一定比例的人民币保证金，然后银行才能开立信用证。

通常信用证应在装运期前一个月开立并到达出口方，以便出口方有足够的时间备货装船。信用证中应说明最大金额、信用证的有效期、汇票的期限，以及应随汇票一起提交的装运单据。

三、信用证的修改或展延

出口方在收到有关信用证后，应仔细审核以确保信用证的规定与合同条款完全相符。如有不符，出口方应在装运前要求进口方对信用证做出必要的修改，否则出口方的汇票就有可能遭到银行拒付。有时由于某种原因，出口方可能无法按合同规定出运货物，这时，出口方应要求进口方展延信用证中的装运期以及信用证自身的有效期。

有时进口方可能未及时开立有关信用证或有关信用证未及时到达出口方，这时出口方应写信给进口方，催其尽快开证。无论是何种原因导致出口方未及时收到有关信用证，出口方在拟写催证信的时候，言语都必须得体，因为催证信的目的是为了促使进口方更好地合作，履行职责。言语不当只会激怒对方，产生不良后果。

因为对信用证的修改或展延既需要时间又花费金钱，所以也是进口方最不愿意遇到的事情，因此在写信要求进口方改证或展延信用证时，应注意礼貌。要求进口方修改信用证的信函应包括以下三个方面的内容。

1. 感谢对方开出的信用证。在开头部分表示感谢并引用信用证的号码、开证行和开证日期等相关信息。

2. 列明不符点，并说明如何修改。在正文部分，逐条列出信用证中存在的不符点，并详细说明如何修改。

3. 在修改函的结束部分，感谢对方的合作，并希望信用证修改书早日开出，以利于继续履约。

展证信的内容应包括以下要点。

1. 提出具体的展证要求，即要求展延多少天或展延到具体某一天。

2. 说明展证的原因和理由。

四、信用证和汇票范本

信用证样本

（以下信用证内容源自我国××陶瓷厂与一塞浦路斯客户所开立并顺利支付的信用证）

TO: BANK OF CYPRUS LTD

LETTERS OF CREDIT DEPARTMENT

NTCOSIA COMMERCIAL OPERATIONS CENTER

INTERNATIONAL DIVISION

TEL:×××××××

FAX:×××××××

TELEX: 2451 & 4933 KYPRIA CY

SWIFT: BCYPCY2N

DATE: 23 MARCH 2010

APPLICATION FOR THE ISSUANCE OF A LETTER OF CREDIT

SWIFT MT700 SENT TO:MT700转送至

STANDARD CHARTERD BANK

UNIT 1-8 52/F ×× SQUARE

×× COMMERCIAL CENTRE,

×× SHEN NAN ROAD EAST,

SHENZHEN 518008–CHINA

渣打银行深圳分行

深南东路×××号

信兴广场××商业大厦52楼1–8单元

电　　话：82461688

:27: SEQUENCE OF TOTAL序列号

1/1 指只有一张电文

:40A: FORM OF DOCUMENTARY CREDIT跟单信用证形式

IRREVOCABLE 不可撤销的信用证

:20DCUMENTARY CREDIT NUMBER信用证号码

00143-01-0053557

:31C: DATE OF ISSUE开证日期

如果这项没有填，则开证日期为电文的发送日期。

:31DATE AND PLACE OF EXPIRY信用证有效期及地点

100622 IN CHINA 2010年6月22日在中国到期

:50: APPLICANT 信用证开证申请人

×××××× NICOSIA 校对地址，应同发票一致

:59: BENEFICIARY 受益人

CHAOZHOU HUALI CERAMICS FACTORY

FENGYI INDUSTRIAL DISTRICT, ×× TOWN, ×× CITY, ××

PROVINCE, CHINA. ××陶瓷洁具厂

:32B: CURRENCY CODE, JAMOUNT 信用证项下的金额

USD***7841,89

:41D:AVAILABLE WITH...BY...议付适用银行

STANDARD CHARTERED BANK

CHINA AND/OR AS BELOW 渣打银行或以下的

BY NEGOTIATION 任何议付行

:42C DRAFTS AT SIGHT 即期汇票

:42A DRAWEE 付款人

BCYPCY2NO10

BANK OF CYPRUS LTD 塞浦路斯的银行名

:43PARTIAL SHIPMENTS 是否允许分批装运

NOT ALLOWED 不可以

:43T:TRANSHIPMENT转运

ALLOWED允许

:44A LOADING ON BOARD/DISPATCH/TAKING IN CHARGE AT/FROM...装船港口

SHENZHEN PORT深圳

:44B:FOR TRANSPORTATION TO 目的港

LIMASSOL PORT发票中无提及

:44C: LATEST DATE OF SHIPMENT最后装船期

100601

:045A DESCRIPTION OF GOODS AND/OR SERVICES 货物/服务描述

SANITARY WARE 陶瓷洁具

F O B SHENZHEN PORT, INCOTERMS 2000 离岸价，××港，INCOMTERMS 2000

:046A DOCUMENTS REQUIRED 须提供的单据文件

*FULL SET (AT LEAST THREE) ORIGINAL CLEAN SHIPPED ON BOARD BILLS OF LADING ISSUED TO THE ORDER OF BANK OF CYPRUS PUBLIC COMPANY LTD, CYPRUS, NOTIFY PARTIES APPLICANT AND OURSELVES, SHOWING

全套清洁已装船提单原件（至少三份），做成以"塞浦路斯银行股份有限公司"
为抬头，通知开证人和我们自己，注明

*FREIGHT PAYABLE AT DESTINATION AND BEARING THE NUMBER OF
THIS CREDIT.
运费在目的港支付，注明该信用证号码

*PACKING LIST IN 3 COPIES.
装箱单一式三份

*CERTIFICATE ISSUED BY THE SHIPPING COMPANY/CARRIER OR THEIR
AGENT STATING THE B/L NO(S) AND THE VESSEL(S) NAME
CERTIFYING THAT THE CARRYING VESSEL (S) IS/ARE: A) HOLDING A
VALID SAFETY MANAGEMENT SYSTEM CERTIFICATE AS PER TERMS OF
INTERNATIONAL SAFETY MANAGEMENT CODE AND B) CLASSIFIED AS
PER INSTITUTE CLASSIFICATION CLAUSE 01/01/2001 BY AN APPROPRIATE
CLASSIFICATION SOCIETY
由船公司或代理出具注明B/L号和船名的证明书，证明他们的船是：
A) 持有根据国际安全管理条款编码的有效安全管理系统证书；和
B) 由相关分级协会根据2001年1月1日颁布的ICC条款分类的

*COMMERCIAL INVOICE FOR USD11, 202, 70 IN 4 COPIES DULY SIGNED
BY THE BENEFICIARY/IES, STATING THAT THE GOODS SHIPPED:
A) ARE OF CHINESE ORIGIN.
B) ARE IN ACCORDANCE WITH BENEFICIARIES PROFORMA INVOICE
NO. HL050307 DATED 10/03/10.
由受益人签署的商业发票总额USD11，202，70一式四份，声明运输的货物：

A) 原产地为中国

B) 同号码为HL050307开立日为2010/03/10的商业发票内容一致

:047A: ADDITIONAL CONDITIONS附加条件

* THE NUMBER AND DATE OF THE CREDIT AND THE NAME OF OUR BANK MUST BE QUOTED ON ALL DRAFTS (IF REQUIRED).

信用证号码及日期和我们的银行名必须体现在所有单据上(如果有要求)

*TRANSPORT DOCUMENTS TO BE CLAUSED: VESSEL IS NOT SCHEDULED TO CALL ON ITS CURRENT VOYAGE AT FAMAGUSTA, KYRENTA OR KARAVOSTASSI, CYPRUS.

运输单据注明：船在其航行途中不停靠塞浦路斯的Famagusta, Kyrenta 或者 Karavostassi港口

*INSURANCE WILL BE COVERED BY THE APPLICANTS.保险由申请人支付

*ALL DOCUMENTS TO BE ISSUED IN ENGLISH LANGUAGE.所有单据由英文缮制

*NEGOTIATION/PAYMENT:UNDER RESERVE/GUARANTEE STRICTLY PROHIBITED. 禁止保结押汇或是银行保函

*DISCREPANCY FEES USD80, FOR EACH SET OF DISCREPANT DOCUMENTS PRESENTED UNDER THIS CREDIT, WHETHER ACCEPTED OR NOT, PLUS OUR CHARGES FOR EACH MESSAGE CONCERNING REJECTION AND/OR ACCEPTANCE MUST BE BORNE BY BENEFICIARIES THEMSELVES AND DEDUCTED FROM THE AMOUNT PAYABLE TO THEM.

对于本信用证下的每套不符单据，将收取不符点费用80美元，无论接受与否，连同我们表示拒绝和/或接受的信息费用一起由受益人承担，并从付款中扣除。

*IN THE EVENT OF DISCREPANT DOCUMENTS ARE PRESENTED TO US AND REJECTED, WE MAY RELEASE THE DOCUMENTS AND EFFECT SETTLEMENT UPON APPLICANT'S WAIVER OF SUCH DISCREPANCIES, NOT WITH STANDING ANY COMMUNICATION WITH THE PRESENTER THAT WE ARE HOLDING DOCUMENTS AT ITS DISPOSAL, UNLESS ANY PRIOR INSTRUCTIONS TO THE CONTRARY ARE RECEIVED.

如果不符单据是向我方提出并遭拒，除非事先收到相反指示，我们将视为申请人放弃修改这个不符点的权利放单并结算。

（即：你如果提交了有不符点的单据并且被银行拒付的话，如果客人接受这些不符点，银行有权把单据发放给客人。）

*TRANSPORT DOCUMENTS BEARING A DATE PRIOR TO THE L/C DATE ARE NOT ACCEPTABLE.

早于信用证开证日期的运输文件不接受

*DIFFERENCE OF USD 3,363.81(T.E.30 PERCENT OF INVOICE VALUE) BETWEEN L/C AMOUNT AND INVOICES AMOUNT REPRESENTS AMOUNT PAID BY APPLICANTS DIRECT TO BENEFICIARIES OUTSIDE THE L/C TERMS WITHOUT ANY RESPONSIBILITY ON OURSELVES AND TO BE SHOWN ON INVOICES AS SUCH. L/C金额跟发票金额之间的USD 3,363.81的差额（相当于发票额的30%）由申请人直接用L/C以外的方式直接支付给受益人，并在发票上予以相应记载。

:71B: CHARGES

BANK CHARGES OUTSIDE CYPRUS

INCLUDING THOSE OF THE REIMBURSING

BANK ARE FOR BEN. A/C. 在塞浦路斯以外银行产生的费用包括支付行的费

用由信用证收益人负担

:48: PERIOD FOR PRESENTATION 单据提交期限

DOCUMENTS MUST BE PRESENTED WITHIN 21 DAYS AFTER B/LADING DATE, BUT WITHIN THE VALIDITY OF THE CREDIT.在信用证有效期内，最迟装运期后21天内向银行提交单据

:49:CONFIRMATION INSTRUCTIONS保兑指示

WITHOUT 不保兑

:53A: REIMBURSING BANK偿付行

BCYPGB2L

BANK OF CYPRUS UK

INTERNATIONAL DEPARTMENT,

87/93 CHASE SIDE, SOUTHGATE N14 5BU

LONDON-UNITED KINGDOM.

:78: INSTRUCTIONS TO THE PAY/ACCEP/NEG BANK 议付行

NEGO OF DOCS THRU BANK OF CHINA LIMITED CHINA IS ALLOWED.PLEASE DEDUCT RROM YOUR PAYMENT TO BENEFICIARIES THE AMOUNT OF USD1,500 REPRESENTING RECORDING FEES.

可通过中国银行议付，请于受益人的账户中扣去USD 1,500作为记录费。

NEGOTIATION BANK TO OBTAIN REIMBURSEMENT FROM OUR ACCOUNT WITH REIMBURSING BANK 3 BUSINESS DAYS FOLLOWING THEIR AUTHENTICATED TELEX/SWIFT ADVICE TO US, STATING A) OUR CREDIT NUMBER, B)AMOUNT CLAIMED, C) VALUE OF DOCUMENTS D)SHIPMENT/DISPATCH DATE AND E)THAT DOCS ARE IN STRICT COMPLIANCE WITH CREDIT TERMS. ON EXECUTION FORWARD TO US,BANK OF CYPRUS PUBLIC COMAPNY LTD, NICOSIA COMMERCIAL OPER. CENTER INTERN. DIV., 10 KYRIACOS MATSI AV. 1082 AY. OMOLOYITES,NIGOSIA, CYPRUS, ALL DOCS IN ONE LOT BY COURIER SERVICE AT BENEFICIARIES EXPENSE.

所有单据应由偿付行于三个工作日内通过快件形式发给我们，费用由受益人承担。

:72: SENDER TO RECEIVER INFORMATION 附言

CREDIT IS SUBJECT TO U.C.P. 2007 本信用证根据跟单信用证统一惯例UCP600（2007年版）开出

I.C.C PUBL. NO.600. SUBJECT TO URR ICC 525.COLLECT YOUR CHARGES FROM BENE.PLEASE ACKN.RECEIPT. CUMSTOMER'S APPROVAL.

汇票样本

BILL OF EXCHANGE						
Draw Under	HSBC BANK PLC, MONTREAL, CANADA		Irrevocable L/C No.		044/3065889	
Date	MAY. 11, 2010	Payable with interest	At		%	
No.	CA20100511	Exchange for	USD31,800.00		Hangzhou	Jun. 30, 2010
	at	×××	Sight of this FIRST of Exchange（Second of Exchange Being unpaid）			
Pay to the order of	HANGZHOU CITY COMMERCIAL BANK, HANGZHOU, CHINA					
The sum of	U.S. DOLLARS THIRTY ONE THOUSAND EIGHT HUNDRED ONLY					
To	HCBC BANK PLC, MONTREAL, CANADA		JIANGXI WEIYUAN IMPORT AND EXPORT CO., LTD.			

　　汇票（Bill of exchange/postal order/draft）是由出票人签发的，要求付款人在见票时或在一定期限内，向收款人或持票人无条件支付一定款项的票据。汇票是国际结算中使用最广泛的一种信用工具，由各银行印制，内容大致相同，是支付货款的凭证，属于有价证券。

　　汇票中的金额和币值必须一致，信用证下的应按其内容进行缮制。

　　信用证项下的汇票应做到单证一致、单单一致、整洁美观，不得有涂改现象。

第二节 支付术语和信用证的信函范例
(Sample Letters Regarding to Payment Terms and L/C)

一、关于支付方式谈判的范例

Dear Sirs,

We have received your letter of May 5 and noted with interest your *intention* of pushing the sale of our TVs in your country.

Although we *are much appreciative of* your efforts to help sell our TVs, we regret being unable to consider your request for payment by D/A 60 days' sight. Our usual practice is to ask for payment by sight L/C.

However, in order to *facilitate* developing the sale of our TVs in your market, we are prepared to accept payment by D/P at sight as a special *accommodation*. That's to say we'll draw on you a documentary draft at sight, through our bank, *on collection basis*, without L/C.

We hope that the above payment terms will be acceptable to you and look forward to receiving your *trail order* in due course.

    Sincerely yours,

二、催开信用证范例

Dear Sir or Madam,

We refer to the 1,500 dozen shirts under our S/C No.TS121 and wish to point out that the time of shipment is approaching, but there is no indication that relevant

L/C covering the above goods is applied. Please ***do your utmost to*** open L/C without delay.

We would like to make it clear that the contents of L/C should ***be in conformity with*** the terms of the contract so as to avoid further ***amendments***.

We are waiting for your earlier favorable reply.

Yours faithfully,

S.C.Johnson & Son Inc.

James Martinsen

General Manager

三、通知已开立信用证范例

Dear Mr. Pan,

We write to inform you that we have now opened the confirmed, irrevocable letter of credit No. 1234 in your favor for USD 3,000 with the ABC Bank, Boston, valid until 30 June.

The letter of credit ***authorizes*** you to draw at 60 days on the bank in Boston for the amount of your invoice after shipment is made. Before accepting the draft, the bank will require you to present the following document: ***Bill of Lading in triplicate, Commercial Invoice, Packing List, Certificate of Insurance*** and ***Certificate of Origin***.

As the season is drawing near, our buyers are in urgent need of the goods. Please arrange shipment of the goods ordered by us upon receipt of the L/C. We would like to stress that any delay in shipping our order will involve us in no small difficulty. We hope that you will let us know at your earliest convenience the name of *the carrying vessel* and its sailing date.

Thank you in advance for your cooperation.

Yours faithfully,

四、要求修改信用证范例

Dear Sirs:

At hand is your L/C No.4 in the amount of $9,000 from Bank of America to cover your order for 10,000 dozen *men's printed handkerchiefs*.

We would like to request the relative L/C be amended to allow *partial shipment* and *transshipment* of said goods due to the *infrequency* of direct steamers to your port of call. Because we find shipment via Hong Kong necessary more often than not, it would be to our benefit to ship available stock on-hand now, instead of waiting for the fulfillment of the entire lot; rendering partial shipment necessary.

This afternoon, we are faxing to amend the relative L/C to read:
"TRANSSHIPMENT AND PARTIAL SHIPMENT ALLOWED."

Please E-mail the amendment to your bank as soon as possible. We have packed on-hand stock for shipment in preparation of your action.

Thank you for your cooperation.

Sincerely yours,

五、重要词句

1. intention n. 意图；目的；意向

e.g. We appreciate your intention on endeavor to enlarge the turnover.

我们感谢贵方努力扩大交易额的意图。

High precision, flexibility, efficiency and reliability are our intention and mission for our customer.

高精确、高灵活度、高效率、高可靠性是我们对客户的目标和使命。

In short, I have no intention of selling my shares in Arsenal for the foreseeable future.

简而言之，在可以预见的未来，我没有打算卖掉我在阿森纳的股份。

2. are much appreciative of 衷心感谢

e.g. Although we are much appreciative of your efforts to help sell our bicycles, we regret being unable to consider your request for payment by D/A 60 days' sight.

虽然我们衷心感谢你方努力推销我们的自行车，我方歉难考虑你方60天远期承兑交单的要求。

We are much appreciative of the help and contribution from our friendly partners, and thank you for your attendance to today's ceremony; we are looking forward to cooperating with you further.

我们衷心感谢朋友们的帮助与贡献，感谢您参加今天的仪式，我们期待今后与您进行更多、更紧密的合作。

3. facilitate vt. 促进；帮助；使容易

e.g. Personnel Management Systems to facilitate the management of personnel information, the staff more easily.

人事管理系统能方便地管理人事信息，使工作人员更加轻松。

China will always be persistent in open and equal trade, and facilitate convenience in trade and investment.

中国将始终坚持开放和公平的贸易，并提供贸易与投资的便利化。

4. accommodation n. 调节；住处，膳宿；和解；预订铺位，方便，乐于助人

e.g. The large volume of trade should entitle us to special accommodation.

大的交易额应使我方有资格得到特殊的照顾。

All such enterprises shall provide the necessary offices and accommodation free of charge.

各此类企业应当免费提供必需的办公场所和食宿。

5. on collection basis 按托收方式

e.g. We'll draw on you by our documentary draft at sight on collection basis.

我们将按托收方式向你方开出即期跟单汇票。

In our export transactions we flexibly apply common international practice and sometimes effect shipment on collection basis.

我方在出口交易中灵活运用国际上通用的做法，有时以托收方式发货。

We agree that payment is made by documentary draft at sight drawn in favor of you on collection basis instead of L/C.

我们同意采用托收的支付方式，开立以你方为受益人的跟单即期汇票来代替信用证的支付方式。

6. trail order 试销订单

e.g. We shall book a trail order with you, provided you will give us a 5% commission.

假如你方给5%的佣金，我方将向你方试订一批货。

This is the trail order, to which trust you will give your very best attention.

If it is satisfactory, we shall probably be abe to see our way to extensive dealings with you.

本次仅为试订，相信贵方会精心安排。如果我们感到满意，今后我们双方可能会有大宗的交易。

We once told you in the letter on 1ˢᵗ December, we would like to order a trail order for 50 "××" brand bicycles.

我方曾在十二月一日信中告知你方，我方愿向你方试订50辆××牌自行车。

7. do your utmost 尽最大努力

e.g. Please do your utmost to hasten shipment.

请尽最大努力加速装运货物。

Please do your utmost to expedite the L/C so that we may execute the order smoothly.

请尽快开立信用证，以便我方顺利执行订单。

8. be in conformity with 与……一致；与……相符

e.g. If not specified on the contract, the supplied goods should be in conformity with state standard and the enterprise standard of our factory.

用户有特殊要求时，经双方协定在合同上注明，否则一律按国家标准以及本厂标准要求供货。

The sellers shall guarantee that the commodity must be in conformity with the quality and specifications specified in this contract and Letter of Quality Guarantee.

卖方须保证货物品质规格必须符合本合同及质量保证书的规定。

9. amendment n. 修正案；修改书；修正 v. amend

e.g. We are enclosing herewith the policy amendments in duplicate .

兹随函附上保险单修改条款一式两份。

Kindly ask the bank to amend credit No. 45 to read: joint bill of lading with credit No. 48 acceptable.

请要求银行将第45号信用证修改为"接受第48号信用证下联运提单"。

10. authorize vt. 批准，认可；授权给；委托

e.g. He confidentially authorized me to act for him while he is abroad.

他信任地委托我在他出国期间代办他的事务。

They sort good products from bad products and authorize the release of the good products.

该部门从质量差的产品中挑出好产品，并批准放行质量好的产品。

11. Bill of Lading B/L 提单

提单：在对外贸易中，提单是运输部门承运货物时签发给发货人的一种凭证。收货人凭提单向货运目的地的运输部门提货，提单须经承运人或船方签字后才能生效。提单也是海运货物向海关报关的有效单证之一。

e.g. Does carrier need to deliver goods by original straight bill of lading?

承运人需凭正本记名提单交付货物吗？

Required documents from seller: Clean on board bill of lading, invoices, packing list, veterinary certificate, certificate of origin.

卖方提交以下单证：已装船清洁提单、发票、装箱单、兽医证书和产地证。

12. in triplicate 一式三份

e.g. The contract has been written in triplicate.

这份合同写成一式三份。

We would like the invoice for this order sent in triplicate.

我们要这份订单的发票，请寄三联来。

13. Commercial Invoice 商业发票

商业发票是出口方向进口方开列的发货价目清单，是买卖双方记账的依据，也是进出口报关交税的总说明。商业发票是一笔业务的全面反映，内容包括商品的名称、规格、价格、数量、金额和包装等，同时也是进口商办理进口报关不可缺少的文件。因此，商业发票是全套出口单据的核心，在单据制作过程中，其余单据均需参照商业发票缮制。

e.g. The declared value should be consistent with the value mentioned in the commercial invoice.

海关申报值必须与所付商业发票的价值相符。

If you fail to produce the normal commercial invoice of this watch, the Customs will assess duty on it ad valorem the market price of identical or similar watch in Hong Kong.

如果你不能出示这块手表的正规商业发票，海关将参照香港市场的相同或类似品的价格予以估价征税。

14. Packing List 装箱单

装箱单是发票的补充单据，它列明了信用证（或合同）中买卖双方约定的有关包装事宜的细节，便于国外买方在货物到达目的港时供海关检查和核对货物，通常可以将其有关内容加列在商业发票上，但是在信用证有明确要求时，就必须严格按信用证约定制作。

e.g. In each case, a detailed packing list in two copies shall be inserted.

每一个包装箱内，均附有详细的装箱单一式两份。

We are greatly embarrassed by your omission to enclose the packing list with other document.

贵方没有把装箱单和其他货运单据一起寄来，这使我们大为其难。

15. Certificate of Insurance 保险凭证

保险凭证，又称"小保单"，指在保险凭证上不印保险条款，实际上是一种简化的保险单。保险凭证与保险单具有同等效力，凡是保险凭证上没有列明的，均以同类的保险单为准。为了便于双方履行合同，这种在保险单以外单独签发的保险凭证主要在以下三种情况下使用。

（1）在一张团体保险单项下，需要给每一个参加保险的人签发一张单独的凭证。

（2）在货物运输保险订有预约合同的条件下，需要对每一笔货运签发单独的凭证。

（3）对于机动车辆第三者责任险，一般实行强制保险。为了便于被保险人随身携带以供有关部门检查，保险人通常出具保险凭证。此外，我国还有一种联合保险凭证，主要用于保险公司同外贸公司合作时附印在外贸公司的发票上，仅注明承保险别和保险金额，其他项目均以发票所列为准。当外贸公司在缮制发票时，保险凭证也随即办妥。这种简化凭证大大节省人力，目前大陆对我国港澳地区的贸易业务也已大量使用。

e.g. Please forward your current "Certificate of Insurance to" us.

请将贵司目前的保险凭证发给我们。

The consignment is insured by our open policy No 405, and we look forward to receipt of your certificate of insurance.

这批货物由我们的405号预约保险单承保，我们等待着收到你公司的保险凭证。

16. Certificate of Origin 原产地证明书

原产地证明书也叫产地证，是证明商品原产地，即货物生产或制造地的一种证明文件，是商品进入国际贸易领域的"经济国籍"，是进口国对货物确定税率待遇、进行贸易统计、实行数量限制（如配额、许可证等）和控制从特定国家进口（如反倾销税、反补贴税）的主要依据之一。原产地证明书一般有三类：第一类是普惠制原产地证明书；第二类是一般原产地证明书；第三类是某些专业性原产地证明书。

e.g. One copy of Certificate of Origin issued by local Chamber of Comerce in one original.

由当地商会签发的货物原产地证明副本一份。

Certificate of origin in two fold indicating that goods are of Chinese origin issued by Chamber of Commerce.

该条款要求由商会签发的产地证一式两份，证明货物的原产地在中国。

17. the carrying vessel 运输船舶，载货船舶

e.g. The age of the carrying vessel chartered by the Seller shall not exceed 15 years.

卖方所租载货船只船龄不得超过15年。

The document quotes the name of the shipper and the carrying vessel, the ports of shipment, destination, and the freight rate.

提单提供了发货人的姓名和运载船舶的船名，装运港及目的港和运费率。

18. men's printed handkerchiefs 男士印花手帕

19. partial shipment 分批装运

分批装运（Partial shipment）又称分期装运（shipment by installment），指一

个合同项下的货物先后分若干期或若干次装运。在国际贸易中，凡数量较大，或受货源、运输条件、市场销售或资金条件所限，有必要分期分批装运、到货者，均应在买卖合同中规定分批装运条款。如为减少提货手续、节省费用，在进口业务中要求国外出口人一次装运货物的，则应在进口合同中明确规定不准分批装运（partial shipment not allowed）条款。

一般来说，允许分批装运和转运对卖方来说比较主动（明确规定分期数量者除外），根据国际商会《跟单信用证统一惯例》的规定，除非信用证做相反规定，可准许分批装运。但是，如果信用证规定不准分批装运，卖方就无权分批装运。

因此为防止误解，如需要分批装运的出口交易，应在买卖合同中对允许分批装运（partial shipment to be allowed）做出明确规定。

e.g. Partial shipment and transshipment are not allowed in your L/C.

你方信用证不允许分批装运和转船。

Unless otherwise instructed partial shipment will be permitted under this credit.

如无另行要求，根据本信用证规定，准许分批装运。

We would request you to amend your L/C to allow partial shipment and transshipment.

我方请求你方修改信用证允许分批装运和转船。

20. transshipment 转船

转船指在远洋运输中，货物装船后允许在中途港换装其他船舶转运至目的港。按照《跟单信用证统一惯例》的规定，如果信用证未明确规定禁止转船，则视为可以转船。

e.g. There are risks of damage to the goods during transshipment.

在转船期间有货物被损坏的风险。

We prefer direct sailings as transshipment adds to the risk of damage and may delay the arrival.

我们宁可要直达船，因为转船增加了受损的危险，而且可能会耽误到货时间。

21. infrequency n. 罕见；很少发生

第三节　信用证和汇票的实用例句

（Useful Sentences on L/C and Bill of Exchange）

以下是一些非常实用的关于支付的例句。

1. Please be noted that, as agreed, the terms of payment for the above order are sight Letter of Credit established within 2 weeks upon the arrival of our Sales Confirmation.

   请注意，上述订单的支付条件经双方同意是以即期信用证方式支付，而信用证必须在收到我们销售确认书后两个星期内开出。

2. We write to inform you that we have now opened the confirmed irrevocable letter of Credit No. 2234 in your favor for USD 3,000 with the ABC Bank, Boston, valid until 30 September.

   现致函告知你方，我们已由波士顿ABC银行开出以你方为受益人的、保兑的、不可撤销的2234号信用证，金额3 000美元，有效期至9月30日。

3. Please arrange shipment of the goods ordered by us upon receipt of the L/C.

   请收到信用证后即刻安排我们所订货物的装运事宜。

4. Seller shall open operative Bank Performance Bond amounting to 2% of the L/C value favoring the Buyer within 5 banking days after receipt of Buyer's operative L/C.

   在收到买方的有效信用证后5个银行工作日内，卖方须发出以买方为受益人的保证金，金额是信用证金额的2%。

5. Please amend L/C No.315 as followed.

   请按下述意见修改第315号信用证。

6. The L/C must reach us not later than May 8 and remain valid twenty days after the date of shipment.

   信用证必须在5月8日前送达我方，并在装运后20天内有效。

7. For payment we require 100% value, irrevocable L/C in our favor with partial shipment allowed clause available by draft at sight.

我们要求用金额为全部货款、允许分批装运、不可撤销的、并以我方为受益人的信用证，凭即期汇票支付。

8. The shipment date is approaching. We have to point out that we shall be unable to effect shipment within the stipulated time unless your L/C reaches us before the end of this week.

   装运日期日益临近。我们必须指出的是，除非你方信用证本周末之前到达我方，否则我们将无法在规定时间内装运。

9. We have received your L/C No.555, but find it contains the following discrepancies.

   我们已收到你方第555号信用证，但发现其中有下列不符之处。

10. Shipment will be effected within 15~20 days after receipt of the relevant L/C issued by your first class bank in our favor upon signing Sales Contract.

    一经签订销售合同，我方将在接到你方一级银行开出的以我方为受益人的信用证之后的15~20天内安排装运。

11. As for our future orders, could you agree to payment by time L/C?

    关于我们今后的订货，你们能同意用远期信用证付款吗？

12. It is not our practice to accept term L/C.

    接受远期信用证不是我们的习惯做法。

13. Payment by L/C will tie up our money and add to expenses .

    用信用证付款将束缚我们的资金并导致开支的增加。

14. We advise your bank to amend L/C no. 125 to read "partial shipment allowed" .

    我们建议贵方银行修改第125号信用证，写进"允许分批装运"字样。

15. As for payment, we require an irrevocable L/C available by draft at sight .

    关于付款方式，我们要求不可撤销的信用证凭即期汇票支付。

16. I know L/C is all right, but could you be more flexible for future dealings?

    我知道，信用证支付是不错，但是未来的交易你能否更灵活一点？

17. We always require L/C for our exports and we pay by L/C for our imports as well.

我们一向要求以信用证支付我们的出口商品，而我们对进口商品也是用信用证付款。

18. We hope you will make shipment upon receipt of our extension of the L/C without further delay.

希望你方一收到我方展期的信用证就立即装运，不得有进一步的延误。

19. Our usual terms of payment are 30% T/T payment in advance and 70% by confirmed sight L/C.

我们通常的付款条件是电汇30%的预付款，其余70%凭保兑的即期信用证支付。

20. We are pleased to inform you that L/C No. 666 issued by the Chartered Bank of Liverpool for our S/C No. 111 has just received.

现高兴地通知，你方由利物浦麦加利银行开出的、用以支付有关我方第111号售货合同的第666号信用证已经收到。

练习题

1. 用合适的单词填空

（1）Payment is to be e ＿＿＿＿ by a confirmed, irrevocable L/C available by draft at sight.

（2）We are drawing on you for this amount at 30 days and sending the shipping documents to the bank for n ＿＿＿＿ .

（3）We assure you that we will honor all your drafts according to the c ＿＿＿＿ .

（4）D ＿＿＿＿ is needed for the opening of an L/C.

（5）On receipt of your r ＿＿＿＿ of USD2,500, we will commence production of your order.

（6）In international trade, the d ＿＿＿＿ of a draft is usually the importer or the importer's bank.

（7）More favorable p ＿＿＿＿ terms will be conductive to the development of our business.

（8）High bank i _____ will increase our import cost.

（9）Considering the size of your order, we agree to pay by i _____ .

（10）They insist that half of the amount be paid in c _____ .

2. 选择最佳答案填空

（1）Payment _____ L/C as contracted.

    A. by   B. will be   C. is by   D. is to be made by

（2）We are considering _____ your terms of payment.

    A. accepted   B. to accept   C. accepting   D. accept

（3）Thank you for your letter of credit No.4567 _____ through the Commercial Bank covering 3,000 sets of computers.

    A. issued   B. issue   C. issuing   D. to issue

（4）Therefore, we have to request you to extend the date of shipment and _____ of the L/C to September 10 and September 30 respectively.

    A. validity   B. valid   C. validate   D. validly

（5）We send our sincere apologies for the delay and trust that it will not cause too much _____ to you.

    A. convenient   B. convenience   C. inconvenience   D. conveniences

（6）The terms of payment are acceptable, but the price is _____ the local market.

    A. out of line with   B. in line with   C. in line   D. line on

（7）It is very kind of you to _____ the period of validity till 12th September.

    A. extent   B. extension   C. extents   D. extend

（8）_____ L/C should be accompanied with shipping documents.

    A. Documentary   B. Clean   C. Irrevocable   D. Confirmed

（9）We regret to have to reject your _____ by L/C at 30 days sight.

    A. proposal of pay   B. suggestion of payment

    C. proposal of paying for   D. suggestion of payable terms

（10）All the documentary letters of credit are operated through _____ .

A. buyers and sellers　　　B. banks

C. commission agents　　　D. freight forwarders

3. 用合适的介词填空

（1）We are thinking _____ placing _____ you a trial order for 500 kegs _____ Iron Nails shipment _____ September/October.

（2）We have only 300 kegs _____ iron nails in stock; therefore we request you to extend the shipment date your L/C _____ the end _____ November.

（3）We wish to call your attention _____ the validity _____ the L/C, since there is no possibility _____ L/C extension.

（4）Please try your best to push the sales _____ machine tools _____ your end.

（5）Owing _____ heavy commitments, we can not consider any fresh business _____ this line.

4. 将下列语句译成中文

（1）As the selling season is approaching, please expedite *establishment of the covering L/C / amendment to L/C no, HN4387.*

（2）The transaction is concluded on FOB basis, so please *delete the insurance clause / amend your L/C to read* "Freight Collect".

（3）Owing to heavy commitments, we regret being unable to deliver the goods in time and shall be grateful if you will *extend the shipment and validity of your L/C to November 15 and November 30 respectively / agree to extend your L/C for one month.*

（4）Owing to the problem of import license, we regret being unable to *meet your request for L/C extension / agree to partial shipment.*

（5）We regret to inform you that *some points in your L/C do not conform to the contract / we haven't received your L/C amendment up to now.*

第九章　装运

Shipment

本章内容提要
本章内容包括运输方式、运输单据、包装条件、装运通知和装运指示等。

本章知识重点
如何撰写信函催装、装船指示、租船订舱、发出装运通知和提出包装要求。

第一节　装运的写作要点
(Introduction on Shipment)

对外贸易的装运环节是十分复杂的。卖方须按合同及相关文件的要求将货物运送到码头或将货物装在远洋货轮上。因此，丰富的装运知识和完整、明确的装运文件是安全、准确、经济地完成装运所必须的。

一、海运提单

当装运货物时，第一步首先要明确运费率，然后应该要求卖方提交正式的海运提单。海运提单是装运的重要单证，有以下三个作用。

1. 充当货物收据。

2. 成为在某种条件下履行某种义务的契约。

3. 成为所述货物所有权的证据。

二、装运通知

装运通知（Shipping advice，Declaration of shipment，Notice of shipment）系卖方向买方发出货物已于某月某日或将于某月某日装运上某船的通知。装运通知可方便买方购买保险、准备提货手续或转售，其内容通常包括货名、装运数量、船名、装船日期、契约或信用证号码等。装运通知大多以电邮方式发出，偶尔也用航邮方式发出。卖方发出此项通知时，有时还附上或另行寄上货运单据副本，以便进口商了解装货内容，并防止货运单据正本迟到时，买方可及时办理担保提货（Delivery against letter of guarantee）。

在装运通知中，卖方应该详细说明合同号码、装运日期、商品名称、货轮名称、离港与到达日期和所附单据，也可以回顾一下交易过程和表达进一步发展业务的愿望。

在装运货物后，按照国际贸易的习惯做法，卖方应立即（一般在装船后3天内）发送装运通知给买方或其指定人，从而方便买方办理保险和安排接货等事宜。如卖方未及时发送上述装船通知给买方而使其不能及时办理保险或接货，卖方就应负责赔偿买方由此而引起的一切损害及（或）损失。

货物装运完后，卖方应该立即通知买方。

撰写装运信函通常有以下目的。

1. 催促早日装运。

2. 修改装运条款。

3. 发出装船通知。

4. 寄送装船单据等。

第二节 装运实务的范例讲解

（Sample Letters on Shipment）

一、催促卖方及时装运的范例

Dear Sirs,

Referring to our order No. 1234 for 1,000 metric tons of *chemical fertilizer*, we would like to draw your attention to the fact that the time of shipment has long been *overdue*.

As the season is rapidly approaching, our buyers are in urgent need of the goods.

We shall much appreciate it if you effect shipment as soon as possible, thus enabling the goods to arrive here in time to catch the *brisk* demand at the start of the season.

We have been involved in much trouble by your delay, therefore we are now requiring you to do your utmost to deliver the first 500 metric tons as soon as possible.

We are looking forward to receiving your *shipping advice* as soon as possible.

Yours faithfully,

二、装运说明范例

Dear Mr. Wu,

We have received your letter about opening the L/C yesterday.

As **stipulated** in the contract, a confirmed irrevocable L/C No. 123, amounting to USD200,000 has been opened this morning through the Bank of America, New York. Since the purchase is made on FOB basis, please arrange shipment of the goods ordered by us on S/S "Prince" without delay.

We believe the above instructions are clear to you and await your shipping advice.

Yours sincerely,

三、包装说明范例

Dear sirs,

The 12,000 bicycles you ordered will be ready for dispatch by 17th December. Since you require them for onward shipment to Bahrain, Kuwait, Oman and Qatar, we are arranging for them to be packed in **seaworthy** containers.

Each bicycle is enclosed in **a corrugated cardboard pack**, and 20 are banned together and wrapped in sheet plastic. A container holds 240 cycles; the whole cargo would therefore comprise 50 containers, each weighing 8 tons. Dispatch can be made from our works by rail to be forwarded from Shanghai harbor. The freight charges from works to Shanghai are USD80 per container, totally USD4,000 for this **consignment**, excluding container hire, which will be charged to your account.

Please let us have your delivery instruction.

Yours faithfully,

Kang Zhuang

General Manager

四、装运通知范例

Dear Sirs,

SUBJ: 4,000 DOZ T-SHIRTS

We are glad to inform you that the above goods under contract No. 34HBSF/1009CN have been shipped on board S/S "SUNFLOWER" which will sail for your port tomorrow.

Enclosed please find one set of shipping documents *comprising*:

1. One non-negotiable copy of B/L

2. One copy of Commercial Invoice

3. One copy of Packing List

4. One copy of Certificate of Origin

We hope the consignment will reach you in good order and look forward to further expansion of our business.

Yours faithfully,

五、重要词句

1. chemical fertilizer 化肥

2. overdue adj. 迟到的；过期的；未兑的

e.g. After orders have been confirmed, please remit within 3 days before the Shipment,if overdue, orders will automatically be canceled.

订单被确认之后，请在3天之内汇款，如果逾期，订单将被自动取消。

First, we send a statement showing the amount which is overdue.

首先，我们发出一份结算单，注明到期应付的金额。

3. brisk adj. 敏锐的，活泼的

e.g. Business is always brisk before Christmas.

圣诞节前生意总是很兴隆。

Brisk market sales were concentrated in food, beverage,household electrical appliances and clothing.

市场销售旺点主要集中在食品、饮料、家电和服装类。

4. shipping advice装船通知

装船通知也叫装运通知，主要指的是卖方在货物装船后发给买方的包括货物详细装运情况的通知，其目的在于让买方做好筹措资金、付款和接货的准备。

e.g. Our shipping advice was mailed to you ten days ago.

我方装船通知10天前就邮寄给贵方了。

Shipping advice is made by the seller with unfixed format.

装船通知单由卖方缮制，没有固定格式。

5. stipulate vi. 规定；保证

e.g. The company fails to pay on the date stipulated in the contract.

该公司没有按合同中规定的日期付款。

The contract stipulates that the seller pays the buyer's legal cost.

合同规定卖方支付买方的诉讼费用。

6. seaworthy adj. 经得起航海的；适于海运的

e.g. Your packing should be seaworthy and be able to withstand the rough handling during transit.

你们的包装必须具有适航性，并能经得起运输途中的粗鲁搬运。

We use standard seaworthy packing for long distance transportation.

我们采用的是适合于远距离海运的标准包装。

Our cartons for canned food are not only seaworthy, but also strong enough to protect the goods from damage.

我方用于包装罐头商品的纸盒不但适用于海运，其牢固性也足以防止商品的损坏。

7. a corrugated cardboard pack 皱纸板包装

e.g. Each bicycle is enclosed in a corrugated cardboard pack, and 20 are banned together and wrapped in sheet plastic.

每辆自行车被放入一个皱纸板组装盒内，并且每20辆用板料塑料包裹。

8. consignment n. 运送；委托；托运；运送的货物

e.g. The consignment should reach you within the next week.

货物将可在下周内抵达贵公司的所在地。

I hope you will take necessary precautions in packing this consignment.

希望这次交货时对包装给予必要的注意。

9. comprise vt. 包含；由……组成

e.g. This risk may comprise both credit and liquidity risk.

这种风险可能包括信用风险和流动性风险。

10. Contents of a shipping advice

■ The date and number of bill of lading

■ The date and number of the contract

■ The names of commodities and their quality and value

■ The name of the carrying vessel

■ The name of the shipping port/loading port

■ The estimated time of departure（ETD）

■ The name of the destination port

■ The estimated time of arrival（ETA）

第三节　提单和装箱单范本
（Samples of B/L and Packing List）

一、提单范本

<table>
<tr>
<td colspan="2" rowspan="2"></td>
<td colspan="3">INTERNATIONAL BILL OF LADING
NOT NEGOTIABLE UNLESS CON-
SIGNED "TO ORDER"
（SPACES IMMEDIATELY BELOW
FOR SHIPPER'S MEMORANDA）</td>
</tr>
<tr></tr>
<tr>
<td colspan="2">SHIPPER/EXPORTER（COMPLETE NAME
AND ADDRESS）
DELING TRADE BV
P. O. BOX 100
3700 GC BUNSEN
HOLLAND</td>
<td colspan="2">BOOKING NO.
HLS410700</td>
<td>BILL OF LADING NO.
SEAU871107100</td>
</tr>
<tr>
<td colspan="2" rowspan="2">CONSIGNEE（COMPLETE NAME AND AD-
DRESS）
TO ORDER</td>
<td colspan="3">FORWARDING AGENT/F M C NO.
ESPOO FINLAND</td>
</tr>
<tr>
<td colspan="3">POINT AND COUNTRY OF ORIGIN
FINLAND</td>
</tr>
<tr>
<td colspan="2" rowspan="2">NOTIFY PARTY（COMPLETE NAME AND
ADDRESS）</td>
<td colspan="3">ALSO NOTIFY-ROUTING & INSTRUCTIONS</td>
</tr>
<tr>
<td colspan="3">FINAL DESTINATION（OF THE GOODS NOT
THE SHIP）</td>
</tr>
<tr>
<td>VESSEL VOY FLAG
LINDOE MAERSK
711E DE</td>
<td>PORT OF TRANSHIP-
MENT
ROTTERDAM, HOLL-
AND</td>
<td>LOADING PIER
/TERMINAL</td>
<td colspan="2">ORIGINAL（S）TO BE RE-
LEASED AT HELSINKI,
FINLAND</td>
</tr>
<tr>
<td>PORT OF DISCHA-
RGE DALIAN</td>
<td>PLACE OF DELIVERY
BY ON-CARRIER</td>
<td colspan="3">TYPE OF MOVE（IF MIXED, USE BLOCK 20
AS APPROPRIATE）
CONTAINER YARD TO CONTAINER YARD</td>
</tr>
<tr>
<td colspan="5">PERTICULARS FURNISHED BY SHIPPER</td>
</tr>
</table>

MKS. & NOS/ CONT. NOS	NO. OF PKGS.	DESCRIPTION OF PACKAGES AND GOODS	GROSS WEIGHT	MEASUREMENT
CH/ × × / × × ------------ DALIAN CHINA	4760	7 × 20'DC CONTAINERS S.T.C. BAGS DEMINERALIZED WHEY POWDER AS PER CONTRACT NO. CH/99/66.908 AS PER SPECIFICATION SHIPPER ON BOARD SEA NOR-DICA 15.09.2009 FROM HEL SINKI SHIPPER LOAD STOWAGE & COUNT FREIGHT PREPAID	121380.00K	

DECLARED VALUE	IF SHIPPER ENTERS A VALUE. CARRIERS "PACKAGE LIMITA-TIONS OF LIABILITY DOES NOT APPLY AND THE AD VALOREM RATE WILL BE CHARGED. "		FREIGHT PAYABLE AT/BY		
FREIGHT CH-ARGES	RATED AS PER	RATE	PREPAID	COLLECT	CURRENCY	RATE OF EX-CHANGE

FREIGHT CH-ARGES	RATED AS PER	RATE	PREPAID	COLLECT	CURRENCY	RATE OF EX-CHANGE
TOTALS						

THE RECEIPT CUSTODY, CARRIAGE AND DELI-VERY OF THE GOODS ARE SUBJECT TO THE TERMS APPEARING ON THE FACE AND BACK-HE REOF AND TO CARRIER'S APPLICABLE TARIFF.	* APPLICABLE ONLY WHEN USED FOR MULTIMODEL OR THROUGH TRAN-SPORTATION
In witness where of 3 original bills of lading all the same tenor and date one of which being accomplished the others to stand void, have been issued by Sea-land Service. Inc. or its designated agent on behalf of itself, other participating carriers, the vessel, her master and owners or charters.	* INDICATE WHETHER ANY OF THE CARGO IS HAZARDOUS MATERIAL UNDER DOT. IMCO OF OTHER REGU-LATIONS AND INDICATE CORRECT COMMODITY NUMBER IN BOX 20.
SEAU871107110 15/09/09	AT.............. HELSINKI......................... BY .... FOR SEA-LAND SERVICE, INC

二、装箱单范本

JIANGXI WEIYUAN IMPORT AND EXPORT CO., LTD.						
206 GUANGMING ROAD, NANCHANG, P.R.CHINA						
TEL:0086-0791-66789832　　FAX:0086-0791-66789833						
PACKING LIST						
To:	KU TEXTILE CORPO-RATION 430 VTRA MO-NTREAL CANADA		Invoice No.:	CA20100428		
			Invoice Date:	MAY. 7, 2010		
			S/C No.:	878932		
			S/C Date:	APR. 10, 2010		
From:	SHANGHAI	To:	MONTREAL			
Letter of Credit No.:	044/3075898	Issued By:	HSBC BANK PLC MONTREAL CANADA			
Date of Issue:	APR. 28, 2010					
Marks and Numbers	Number and kind of pac-kage Descrip-tion of goods	Quantity	Package	G.W.	N.W.	Meas.
KU S/C No.:878932 Style No.: UK 858 Port of destination: MONTREAL Carton No.: 1-1000	MEN'S JEC-KET SHIPPED IN 1 × 20'FCL.	10,000PCS	1,000CTNS	25,000 KGS	22,000 KGS	91.2M^3
	TOTAL:	10000PCS	1000CTNS	25000KGS	22000KGS	91.2M^3
SAY TOTAL:	ONE THOUSAND CARTONS ONLY.					
	JIANGXI WEIYUAN IMPORT AND EXPORT CO., LTD. 路波					

练习题

1. 用合适的词语填空

（1）When making a s _____ , the first step is to ascertain the freight rate.

（2）We trust that you will make all necessary arrangements to d _____ the goods on time.

（3）As there are few direct s _____ to your port, we trust that partial shipment is satisfactory to make it easier for us to get the goods ready for shipment.

（4）The duplicate shipping d _____ including bill of lading, invoice, packing list and inspection certificate were airmailed to you today.

（5）We are disappointed to learn of the d _____ in shipment of our order.

2. 选择最佳答案填空

（1）The _____ of the S/C and order should be printed on cases to be shipped in addition to other shipping marks.

　　A. numeral　　B. figure　　C. number　　D. numbers

（2）It is important that shipment _____ before the end of this month.

　　A. will be effected　　B. must be effected

　　C. can be effected　　D. be effected

（3）We find that your L/C needs _____ .

　　A. to amend　　B. being amended　　C. amending　　D. to be amending

（4）We are grateful _____ you _____ your early reply.

　　A. to, for　　B. to, to　　C. for, to　　D. for, for

（5）Our customers are pressing us _____ ship the goods on time.

　　A. to　　B. for　　C. that we　　D. on

3. 翻译下列语句

（1）The shipment has arrived in good condition.

（2）As soon as the shipment is arranged, we will send you our Shipping advice containing all the particulars of the goods.

（3）I'm sorry to advise you that we are unable to give you a definite date of shipment for the time being.

（4）Please quote us your freight rate and let us have any information of your sailing.

（5）On perusal, we find that transshipment and partial shipment are not allowed.

（6）由于我们急需这些货物，请收到我们的信用证后赶快装运。

（7）请贵方装运下列货物，交货期不迟于6月10日。

（8）我们在包装和装运时格外小心，所以货物抵达贵处时肯定完好无损。

（9）该货物可以立即交付，准备明天装船。

（10）我们希望更改交货日期不会给你方带来太多的不便。

4. 翻译如下装运信函

Dear sir/Madam,

Thank you for your letter of 18th March requiring earlier delivery of goods under your Purchase Contract No. 588.

We have contacted the shipping company and have been informed that there is no space on ships sailing from here to your port before 20th May. So we regret that we are unable to advance shipment.

We will, however, make sure that the goods are shipped within the contract time.

Yours faithfully,

第十章　保险

Insurance

本章内容提要
本章内容涉及保险的主要险种、保险条款、请求代办保险和修改保险条件。

本章知识重点
如何撰写信函要求代办保险、要求修改保险条件以及对上述信函的回复，重点掌握有关主要险种、保险术语的特殊表达。

第一节　保险的写作要点

（Introduction on Insurance）

在国际贸易业务中，海上保险是不可缺少的。业务量最大、涉及面最广的海上保险是海洋运输货物保险。海洋运输货物保险条款所承保的险别分为基本险别和附加险别两类。

一、基本险别

基本险别有平安险（Free from Particular Average，缩写为F.P.A）、水渍险（With Average or With Particular Average，缩写为W.A or W.P.A）和一切险（All Risk，缩写为A.R.）三种。

1. 平安险

平安险的责任范围：（1）被保货物在运输过程中，由于自然灾害造成整批货物的全部损失或推定全损，被保货物用驳船运往或远离海轮的，每一驳船所装货物可视为一整批；（2）由于运输工具遭受意外事故造成货物全部或部分损失；（3）在运输工具已经发生意外事故的情况下，货物在此前后又在海上遭受自然灾害落海造成的全部或部分损失；（4）在装卸或转运时，由于一件或数件货物落海造成的全部或部分损失；（5）被保人对遭受承保范围内的货物采取抢救、防止或减少货损的措施而支付的合理费用，但以不超过该批被救货物的保险金额为限；（6）运输工具遭难后，在避难港由于卸货所引起的损失以及在中途港、避难港由于卸货、存仓以及运送货物所产生的特别费用；（7）共同海损的牺牲、分摊和救助费用；（8）运输合同订有"船舶互撞责任条款"，根据该条款规定应由货方偿还船方的损失。

2. 水渍险

水渍险的责任范围：除平安险的各项责任外，还负责被保货物由于自然灾害造成的部分损失。

3. 一切险

一切险的责任范围：除平安险和水渍险的各项责任外，还负责被保货物在运输途中由于一般外来原因所造成的全部或部分损失。

二、附加险别

附加险别是基本险别责任的扩大和补充，它不能单独投保，附加险分为一般附加险和特别附加险。

1. 一般附加险

一般附加险有11种，它包括偷窃、提货不着险（Theft, Pilferage and Non-delivery，缩写为T.P.N.D），淡水雨淋险（Fresh Water and/or Rain Damage，缩写为F.W.R.D），短量险（Risk of Shortage in Weight），渗漏险（Risk of Leakage），混杂、沾污险（Risk of Intermixture and Contamination），碰损、破碎险（Risk of Clash and Breakage），串味险（Risk of Odor），受潮受热险（Sweating and Heating Risk），钩损险（Hook Damage Risk），包装破裂险（Breakage of Packing Risk），锈损险（Risk of Rust）。

2. 特殊附加险

特殊附加险包括交货不到险（Failure to Deliver Risk），进口关税险（Import Duty Risk），舱面险（On Deck Risk），拒收险（Rejection Risk），黄曲霉素险（Aflatoxin Risk），卖方利益险（Seller's Contingent Risk），出口货物到我国香港（包括九龙）或澳门存仓火险责任扩展条款（Fire Risk Extension Clause for Storage of Cargo of Destination Hongkong Including Kowloon, or Macao），海运战争险（Ocean Marine Cargo War Risk）以及罢工险（Strikes Risk）等。

三、保险信函写作及保险单范本

当撰写保险信函时，以下几点应提及：被保险的商品名称、商品的价值、目的港、装运货物的货轮名称，以及要求的保险种类。撰写保险信函时要尽量避免使用难于理解的词汇，在行文时要注意礼貌礼节。

保险单范本

××保险公司

×× INSURANCE COMPANY

总公司设于×× ××年创立

Head Office: ×× Established in ××

| 发票号码 | 保险单 | 保险单号次 |
| Invoice No. | INSURANCE POLICY | Policy No. |

××保险公司（发下简称本公司）

This Police of Insurance witnesses that ×× Insurace

Company of China (hereinafter called "The Company")

根据

at the request of

（以下简称被保险人）的要求，由被保险人

(hereinafter called the "Insured")and in consideration of the agreed premium

向本公司缴付约定的保险费，按照本保险单

paying to the Company by the Insured, Undertakes to insure the undermentioned

承保险别和背面所载条款与下列特款承保

Goods in transportation subject to the conditions of this Policy as per Clauses

下述货物运输保险，特立本保险单。

printed overleaf and other special clauses attached hereon.

标记 Marks & Nos	包装及数量 Quantity	保险货物项目 Description of Goods	保险金额 Amount Insured

总保险金额：

Total Amount Insured

保费 费率 装载运输工具

Premium as arranged Rate as arranged Per conveyance S.S

开航日期   自   至

Sig on or abt   From   To

承保险别

Conditions

所保货物，如遇出险，本公司凭本保险单及其他有关证件给付赔款。

Claims, if any, payable on surrender of this Policy together with other relevant documents.

所保货物，如发生本保险单项下负责赔偿的损失事或事故，应立即通知本公司下述代理人查勘。

In the event of accident whereby loss or damage may result in a claim under this policy immediate notice applying for survey must be given to the company's Agent as mentioned hereunder.

××保险公司

××INSURANCE CO.

赔款偿付地点

Claim payable at

日期

Date

第二节 保险实务的范例讲解
(Sample Letters on Insurance Practices)

一、买方询问保险的范例

Dear Mr. Beare,

With regard to our order of 200 *porcelains*, we have issued an irrevocable L/C at sight which takes your company as the beneficiary.

You will be advised by Shanghai Branch of the Bank of China very soon. So you can prepare for the production and shipment without any concern.

There is another issue we want to request here. As we know, the price that has been stipulated in both of the S/C and L/C is based on CFR term, and hence insurance lies within our responsibilities. For the sake of convenience we wonder whether you could have the goods insured, on behalf of us, against All Risks, Breakage and War Risk for 110% of the invoice value at your end. The *premium charge* is, of course, *for our account*.

Hope this request will be met with your approval.

Yours faithfully,

二、回复买方询问保险范例

Dear Mr. Zhao,

This is to acknowledge the receipt of your letter informing the opening of the L/C and requesting us to cover insurance for *the captioned goods* on your behalf.

We are willing to accept your request. Before completing the shipment we will insure the consignment with the local branch of the PICC as per the risks coverage and insured value you mentioned. Then we will send you the insurance policy together with *a debit note* for the premium fee.

We hope we could serve your company to your satisfaction.

Yours faithfully,

三、要求修改保险条款范例

Dear Sirs,

We wish to refer you to our Order No.3434 for 600 shirts which is placed on a CIF basis.

In accordance with the contract No. 6789, you are requested to insure the goods against All Risks at invoice value plus 10%. But now we desire to have the shipment insured for 120% of the invoice value.

We sincerely hope that our request will not bring much trouble to you.

Faithfully yours,

四、回复要求修改保险条款的范例

Dear Sirs,

This is to acknowledge receipt of your letter dated 3th March requesting us to effect insurance on the captioned shipment for 120% of the invoice value.

We regret our inability *in complying with* your request because it's our usual practice to insure our customers on their orders for 110% only against All Risks. As a result, the extra premium involved will be for buyer's account. In the proper case, the difference between 120% and 110% should be at your cost.

Upon receipt of your approval, we will effect insurance for the captioned goods without any delay.

Faithfully yours,

五、重要词句

1. porcelain n. 瓷；瓷器

2. premium charge 保费

e.g. Premium is a one-time charge, bank charges and the rebate is a one-time payment as well.

保费是一次性收的，给银行的手续费和回扣也是一次性付的。

3. for one's account 费用由某人承担

e.g. The extra packing costs would be for the buyer's account.

额外的包装费用应由买方负担。

4. the captioned goods 标题所述货物；标的物

e.g. The captioned goods you shipped per S. S. "Yellow River" on May 14 arrived here yesterday.

贵方5月14日通过"黄河"号轮船运送的标题所示货物于昨日抵达本地。

The captioned goods are urgently needed, so we wish to receive your proforma invoice by return.

我们急需标题所提到的商品，因此希望尽快收到贵方的形式发票。

5. a debit note收款单

e.g. We enclose a debit note on which the charges are billed .

随函寄去收款单一份，各项费用均已列明。

We shall refund the premium to you as soon as your debit note reaches us, or, if you like, you may draw on us a sight draft.

一收到你方收款单，我方将返还保险费，或者如果你方愿意，也可以开出即期汇票向我方收款。

6. In accordance with按照

e.g. Master all department activities in accordance with company strategy.

根据公司战略掌握各部门所有的活动。

In the "customer first" service purposes, we will, in accordance with the needs of the customers, supply most professional design, production and sales information.

本着"客户至上"的服务宗旨，我们将会根据客户的需要提供最专业的设计、生产和销售的资讯。

7. in complying with答应、符合

e.g. My boss hesitated not a moment in complying with her request.

我的老板毫不犹豫地答应了她的请求。

In Complying with Uruguay Round Agreements to realize economic globalization and trade liberalization, the unbalanced development among countries arouses the unbalanced trade benefits.

在以执行乌拉圭回合协议为核心内容的这一轮经济全球化和贸易自由化过程中，各国经济发展不平衡引起了经济贸易利益分配的不平衡。

第三节 保险单的实用例句
（Useful Sentences on Insurance Policy）

以下是一些非常实用的关于保险的例句。

1. According to the international practice, we do not insure against T.P.N.D risks unless they are called for by the buyers.

   按照国际惯例，除非买方要求，我们通常不投保偷窃、提货不着险。

2. Thank you in advance for making your rates available to us immediately.

   请贵公司立即将你们所使用的费率告知，我们在此预谢。

3. The extra premium is for the buyer's account, should additional risks be covered.

   如果投保附加险，额外保费由买方承担。

4. For this shipment, our client requests you to insure against All Risks and War Risk.

   对于这批货物，我方客户要求你们投保一切险和战争险。

5. Breakage is a special risk, for which an extra premium will be charged.

   破碎险是特别险，要收取额外保费。

6. This kind of risk is coverable at a premium of 1%.

   这种险的保险费率是1%。

7. Please insure the goods for RMB500,000 against All Risks and War Risk.

   请为货物投保人民币50万元的一切险和战争险。

8. We only issue F.P.A, W.P.A and All Risks, but we could add special coverage if a customer requires.

   我们仅有平安险、水渍险和一切险，如果客户需要的话，我们可以另加特别附加险。

9. Enclosed are details of packing and values. Please quote us a rate covering All Risks from port to port.

   兹附有关货物的包装情况及货价的详细凭证，请报港至港一切险费率。

10. We shall be glad to know whether you can undertake insurance of wine against All Risks, including Breakage and Pilferage.

    我们希望知道你们是否可为葡萄酒承保全损险，包括破损险和偷窃险。

11. Cargo insurance is a major business item of our company.

    货物保险是我们公司的一个主要业务项目。

12. Please give us the policy rates for F.P.A coverage.

    请给我方报平安险的保险费率。

13. Please insure us the goods detailed below.

    请替我方投保下列各项货物。

14. We'd like to cover the Risk of Breakage for this lot of goods.

    我们想为这批货物投保破碎险。

15. We usually effect insurance against All Risks and War Risk for the invoice value plus 10% for the goods sold on CIF basis.

    对于按CIF条款成交的货物，我们通常按发票金额加10%将货物投保一切险和战争险。

16. We agree to your request to insure the shipment for 120% of the invoice value, but the premium for the difference between 120% and 110% should be for your account.

    我们同意你方要求按发票金额的120%替货物投保，但是120%和110%之间的保险费差额将由你方负担。

17. We shall insure against W.P.A at your cost.

    我们将投保水渍险，费用由你方负担。

18. Upon receipt of your approval, we will effect insurance for the captioned goods without any delay.

    一旦收到你方来函表示同意，我方将为标题所述货物立即投保。

19. Premium will be added to invoice amount together with freight charges.

    保险费将连同运费合并在发票金额之内。

20. We shall take our insurance at this end under open policy.

    我们将在我地办理预约投保。

练习题

1. 用合适的介词填空

（1）The validity date of the L/C should be extended _____ July 30.（to/on）

（2）Please insure _____ 10% above invoice value.（for/at）

（3）We shall provide such insurance _____ your cost.（on/at）

（4）The business is on FOB basis, so the insurance should be effected _____ the buyers.（by /at）

（5）This risk is coverable _____ a premium of 3%.（on/at）

（6）An insurance claim should be submitted _____ the insurance company as promptly as possible.（to/at）

（7）We shall cover for T. P. N. D _____ your order.（for/on）

（8）As usual, the goods have been insured _____ W.P.A terms.（on/in）

（9）Please arrange insurance on the goods _____ All Risks.（against/with）

（10）We shall arrange insurance _____ your behalf.（for/on）

2. 选择最佳答案填空

（1）We shall _____ insurance against All Risks.

　　A. insure　　B. make　　C. underwrite　　D. have

（2）We often insure shipment for the invoice value _____ 10%.

　　A. adding　　B. with　　C. over　　D. plus

（3）If you desire to _____ your goods against All Risks, we can provide such coverage at a slightly higher premium.

　　A. guarantee　　B. guard　　C. cover　　D. protect

（4）The buyer will pay the extra premium if he requests that insurance _____ more than 110%.

　　A. covered　　B. be covered　　C. cover　　D. to be covered

（5）The additional premium _____ by us.

　　A. is born　　　　B. will be taken

　　C. will be borne　　D. will be undertaken

（6）We _____ receipt of your letter of April 3, 2002.

      A. acknowledge   B. inform   C. are   D. have

（7）The car I bought last week _____ me $ 50,000.

      A. cost   B. spend   C. costs   D. spent

（8）The insurance company is responsible _____ the claims.

      A. to   B. on   C. with   D. for

（9）The W.P.A covers _____ risks than F.P.A.

      A. less   B. more   C. wider   D. fewer

（10）After loading the goods on board the ship, you must arrange with the insurance company to have them _____.

      A. insure   B. to be insured   C. to insure   D. insured

3. 翻译以下内容

（1）All Risks

（2）insurance policy

（3）invoice value

（4）conclude on CIF basis

（5）marine insurance

（6）保险凭证

（7）保险代理人

（8）水渍险

（9）平安险

（10）保险费率

4. 将如下信函译成中文

Dear Sir/Madam,

We have received with thanks your quotation for 400 bales of cotton on CIF terms.

As our usual practice we prefer to receive quotations on CFR terms.

As you know, we have taken out an open policy with the People's Insurance Company of China. All we have to do when a shipment is sent is to advise them of the particulars. Furthermore, we keep very good relationship with them. We regularly receive from them premium rebate.

In the meanwhile, we should be grateful if you could supply us with full details regarding the coverage handled by Lloyd's Insurance Company, London for our reference.

We await your early reply.

Yours faithfully,

第十一章　投诉、索赔和理赔

Complaint, Claim and Settlement

本章内容提要
本章内容包括投诉、争议、索赔和理赔。

本章知识重点
如何撰写信函向出口商、承运人和保险公司提出投诉与索赔要求，回复索赔要求，了解各种导致损失的原因的表达方法。

第一节 索赔与回复的写作要点
（Introduction on Claim and Its Reply）

一、对索赔与理赔的介绍

索赔在法律上的含义是"维护权利"。买卖双方通过订立合同，各自都要求承担合同中规定的义务，同时享有一定的权力。在实际履行中，一方未能履行或未能全部履行自己的义务，即构成违约。另一方则可以根据合同赋予的权利向违约方提出损害赔偿的要求，即索赔。索赔涉及的对象除合同的当事人外，有时还会涉及承运人、保险人及银行。索赔必须在合同规定的有效期内提出（一般规定是在货到后30天内提出），否则违约方可以不受理。《联合国国际货物销售合同公约》规定，如买卖合同未规定索赔期限，且到货检验又不易发现货物缺陷的，则买方先例索赔权的最长期限为实际收到货物起不超过两年。违约方受理对方的赔偿要求称作理赔。在国际贸易中，索赔和理赔的情况是经常发生的。即使双方很小心，仍然会有申诉和索赔的情况出现。解决争议，达成索理赔协议，须经双方平等协商，从而理顺贸易关系，解决业务纠纷。

二、索赔与理赔信函的写作

对于索赔、理赔函电的拟写，索赔方要实事求是，据理力争；理赔方要澄清事实，分辨是非，这样就有利于纠纷的妥善解决。反之，双方措辞激烈、剑拔弩张、咄咄逼人、或抱有非分奢望，或赖账狡辩，不仅无助于纠纷的解决，最终很可能会适得其反。

理赔索赔信函通常包括如下内容。

开头：说明写信的原因——申诉或索赔的事件。

正文：具体介绍发生的事情，如有证据可提供；提出自己的要求，如要求退货，赔款等。

结尾：希望满足自己的要求，表达合作的意愿等。

接受申诉或理赔的回信要点如下。

开头：说明收到来信并表示很遗憾。

正文：对对方信中提及的事情加以解释、调查，并针对对方的要求给予答复。

结尾：表示道歉和进一步合作的希望。

表示不能接受申诉或索赔的回信要点如下。

开头：说明收到来信并表示遗憾。

正文：对事件进行调查，加以解释，说明原因和提出证据说明不能负责。

结尾：期望以后有合作的机会，或再次表示遗憾。

每封信件的具体内容会有变化，需要根据实际情况加以调整。

第二节　索赔与理赔的范例讲解
（Sample Letters on Claim and Its Acceptance）

一、对误发货的投诉信范例

Dear Sirs,

Thank you for your delivery of table cloth which we ordered on October 12. To our regret, *on inspection*, we found that the goods do not *conform to* the samples. We wish to invite your attention to the following points:

1. The colors of the cloths are different to your original sample.

2. The finish is unsatisfactory.

We are returning two of these *by separate mail* and would like you to *replace* the whole in correct color immediately, *as we are in urgent need of them*. Concerning the airfreight, we agree to pay the extra costs for *airfreight*. However, your costs for packing and insurance must have been lower for air cargo and we *request you to take this fact into consideration* and bear some part of the airfreight charges.

We think that we may be able to *dispose of* them and await your reply as to whether you agree to our proposal.

Yours faithfully,

二、对投诉致歉的范例

Dear Sirs,

We hasten to reply to your letter March 19. We have in the first place to apologize to you for the most unfortunate error that has occurred in the execution of your order. We are completely at a loss to understand how this mistake could not be found out as all goods are checked and cross-checked at our forwarding department.

It is the first case in all these years that we have caused you to complain about and we shall *take every care to* avoid such an error in the future. We are really sorry for your inconvenience. *In order not to give you further trouble we have air-mailed another lot of the table cloth today and they will reach you within a week.*

Please debit us with your returning charges and others. Let us *assure you that* we shall take every care and such an accident like this should never occur again.

Yours faithfully,

三、对货物受损的索赔范例

Dear Sirs,

"East Wind" ——2,500 Tons of Maize

The above shipment is covered by Bill of Lading No. 23/456 issued by your office in Kobe.

Upon being taken delivery, the cargo was found to have been seriously wetted by fresh water and putrefied. *The outturn report* gives a total weight of 2,600 *metric tons.*

According to the survey by *the China Commodity Inspection Bureau*, the over-weigh is *in consequence of* excessive moisture in the maize. The fresh water entered the hold through the ventilators which the crew had *failed to close up* when the ship met with boisterous weather on the way. This is definitely a case of negligence.

As the cargo is no longer fit for human consumption, we must ask that you compensate us for the loss.

We are *holding the cargo at your disposal* and look forward to your prompt reply.

Yours faithfully,

四、接受索赔范例

Dear Sirs,

<u>Your Claim No. 236</u>

With reference to your claim No. 236 for a short weight of 45M / T Soybean, we wish to express our much regret over the unfortunate incident.

After a check-up by our staff, it was found that the Case 16 had been sent to you *by mistake*. This case was to be sent to another customer, *with 30 bags in it which was less 15 bags than yours*. We apologize for the inconvenience you have sustained and assure you that we shall be careful never to make such a mistake again.

In view of our friendly business relations, we are prepared to *meet your claim* for the short weight of 45M / T. *Enclosed is a check for* USD 259, which will *cover*

> ***the whole loss of*** yours.
>
> We trust that the arrangement we have made will satisfy you and look forward to receiving your further orders.
>
> Yours faithfully，

五、重要词句

1. Structure of a letter for complaint

（1）Beginning paragraph: referring to the terms agreed by the two parties.

　　开头：提及双方的协议条款。

（2）Transitional paragraph: the reasons of complaining and the solution you hope.

　　中间的主要内容：写抱怨的因由和你希望的解决方式。

（3）Ending paragraph: hoping for an early solution.

　　结尾：希望早日得到解决。

2. on inspection　通过检查 = when inspected

e.g. You will find on inspection thereof that there be a balance in your favour of RMB100, 000 for which we enclose check.

　　经检查账目，发现贵方应收往来差额款10万元，为此我们同函奉上支票一张。请查收。

3. conform to / with vi 与某物一致，符合，相似

e.g. Replace the defective goods with new ones which conform to the specifications, quality and performance stipulated in this contract.

　　用全新的符合本合同规定的规格、质量和功能的货物更换有缺陷的货物。

4. airfreight　n. 空中货运（费）

e.g. The freight charges include airfreight, handling, airport terminal, documentation charges, etc.

空运费用包括机场理货费、空港费、文件单证费等。

5. by separate mail 通过分别邮寄的方式；另行邮寄

e.g. I'll send it by surface mail. 我将用平邮方式把它寄出去。

We now work on a new catalog, which you will shortly receive by separate mail.

目前我方正在赶印新的商品目录，将另函附邮，不日即可收到。

We send you by separate mail a copy of Certificate of Quality No. 123, please acknowledge receipt.

现另邮寄去第123号品质证明书一份，请确认收到。

6. replace 替换，以……代替

e.g. The shopkeeper said he would replace the radio set if we were not satisfied.

店主说如果我们对那台收音机不满意的话，他可以给我们换一台。

replacement n. 代替，代替物

We want your delivery of the goods to be exact to the sample. Any replacement of the goods will not be accepted.

我们希望你们发送的货物与样品完全相同，我们将不接受任何货物替代物。

7. as we are in urgent need of them. 因为我们急需要用这些货物。

8. Request you to take this fact into consideration. 敬请贵方考虑这一事实。

9. dispose vt. 安排，处理，控制

　dispose of 处理，卖掉，安排

e.g. The firm was forced to dispose of（sell）the unsellable goods.

　　公司被迫处理了那些滞销货。

10. It is the first case in all these years that we have caused you to complain about.

这些年来这是我们第一次给你们造成索赔的案例。

11. take every care to do 做某事多加小心，做事当心

e.g. The shipping company should take care to avoid any loss and damage of the cargo.

船公司应该小心以免造成货物丢失或破损。

12. In order not to give you further trouble we have air mailed another lot of the table cloth today and they will reach you within a week.

为了不给你方带来更多的麻烦，我方已于今日航邮另外一批台布，一星期内将到达贵方。

13. assure somebody that... 向某人保证……，使某人确信、放心

e.g. The seller assured us that they would arrange the shipment in due time.

卖方向我们保证一定会按时安排装运。

14. lodge（raise, file, put in...）a claim against sb. for sth. 对……向某人提出索赔

15. to claim ... with sb. for sth. 因……向某人提出索赔

e.g. This damage was due to the rough handling by the shipping company. You should claim with them for recovery of the loss.

这种损失是由于运输公司的操作不当造成的，你们应当向他们提出索赔。

16. The above shipment is covered by Bill of Lading No. 23/456 issued by your Office in Kobe.

上述装载货物是你神户分公司签发的第23/456号提单项下的货物。

17. upon being taken delivery. 在货物被提取时

upon doing sth. 就在某场合或某事之后

Upon receipt of your relevant L/C, we will get the goods ready for shipment.

一收到你们的相关信用证，我们将立即将货物备妥待运。

18. take delivery of goods... 提取……，收到……

e.g. We found that some lots have been slightly damaged when we took delivery of the consignment.

我们在提取货物时发现有些批次轻微受损。

19. the cargo was found to have been seriously wetted by... 货物已经严重受潮

e.g. The damaged goods were found to have been repaired when they were resent to us.

当我们收到再次寄来的受损货物时发现它们已经被修理好了。

20. outturn report   卸货报告

   outturn clause   卸货数量条款

   outturn sample   货物送达时所取的样本

21. metric ton 公吨

1公吨（Tonne, Metric ton）= 1 000公斤，1吨（Ton）=1 016公斤（Br）或907.2公斤（US）。

公吨是公制的单位，在英文中原本的表达法为Tonne或者Metric ton。由于用公吨的人太多，故常把Metric ton缩略为Ton。国外客户说Ton的时候，有可能是指Metric ton。中国人说吨，其实指的都是公吨，因为中国采用公制。（我们说1吨等于1 000公斤，也证明了我们所说的吨，其实是公吨。）

吨（原本意义上的吨）是英制单位，英文中用Ton表示。英国和美国对Ton的定义不同。在英国1Ton等于1 016公斤，因此英国的吨又称为Long ton（长吨）；在美国1Ton等于907公斤，因此美国的吨又称为Short ton（短吨）。

为避免混淆，建议公司相关人员与客户洽谈的时候都统一用Metric ton这种说法，写合同时更应如此。

22. according to...根据……

e.g. Meet with suppliers according to schedule.

   按照计划与供应商会面。

   But we also sell steel according to specifications or for special purposes.

   但我们也销售按照规格供应的或作特殊用途的钢材。

23. The China Commodity Inspection Bureau   中国商品检验局

24. in consequence of   由于……的缘故

e.g. The market is advancing in consequence of the price of Light Shoes which is fair.

   由于轻便鞋的价格比较公正，因此这个市场发展良好。

   The new product sells fast in consequence of its reasonable price and good quality.

   由于价格合适、质量好，所以这个新产品销售很好。

25. fail to close up   没有关闭

fail to do sth.　未能做某事，忘记做某事

e.g. When marketers do not understand and appreciate the values, tastes, geography, climate, superstitions, religion, or economy of a culture, they fail to capture their target market.

营销商不了解和重视一种文化的价值观、品位、地理、气候、迷信、宗教以及经济等，他们就把握不住他们的目标市场。

26. hold/put sth. at one's disposal　把某事交给某方处理或安排

at one's disposal　由某人使用（或支配处理）

e.g. We put the business at the exclusive agent's disposal in Japan.

我们将业务交给在日本的独家代理处理。

That leaves adjusting tax rebates for exporters as one of the few policy tools at Beijing's disposal to help address exporters' woes.

调整出口退税是北京可以掌握的少数几个可以帮助出口商缓解困境的政策工具之一。

27. by mistake　过失，弄错

e.g. It was found that the Case 16 had been sent to you by mistake.

我们发现发送给你们的16号箱发错了。

We apologize that we made mistake on the shipping of No. 46 container. After investigation, we find out that we put the goods together by mistake when shipping.

有关第46号集装箱错运货物一事，我们在此向贵公司致歉。经调查，发现装运时误将货物同放，所以出此错误。

28. With 30 bags in it which was less 15 bags than yours.

里面装有30袋大豆，比贵方的少15袋。

29. in view of　由于，考虑到，有鉴于

e.g. In view of our long-term cooperation relationship, we only returned the inferior shipment to you without lodging a claim on compensation.

考虑到我们长期的合作关系，我们仅将劣质货品退回而没有要求额外赔偿。

In view of our long and friendly relations, we accept the payment terms you proposed.

鉴于我们的长期友好关系，我们接受了你方提出的付款条件。

30. meet one's claim 满足某人的索赔

e.g. Their new model of car is so popular that they have had to open a new factory to meet the demand.

他们的新型汽车非常流行，他们不得不再开一家新工厂以满足需求。

We are prepared to meet your claim for the 30 tons short weight.

我们准备接受你们对30吨短重的索赔。

31. Enclosed is a check for which... 随函寄去一张面值……的支票

32. cover the loss 弥补损失

e.g. The contract stimulates that the insurance doesn't cover the loss in the case.

合同规定，该案例中的损失不在保险理赔范围中。

第三节 索赔的实用例句
（ Useful Sentences Related to Claims ）

以下是一些关于索赔的典型例句。

1. We presume the goods in case No.5 to be of inferior quality.

我们猜想，第5号箱中货物质量低次。

2. Did you check the quality of each dispatch?

每批发出的货物，你们都检查过质量吗？

3. After checking the goods against your invoice, we discovered a considerable shortage in number.

经过按发票查对之后，我们发现数量少了很多。

4. We have already lodged a claim against the underwriters for STG.665 for damage in transit.

由于货物在运输途中受损，我们已经向保险商提出索赔665英镑。

5. We claim USD 3,000 for short shipment on the 50 tons Peanuts ex S.S. "MAYFLOWER".

由"五月花"轮运来的50吨花生，由于短装，我方提出索赔3 000美元。

6. We request to extend the time limit for claim on the above shipment to the middle of May.

我们要求对上述货物的索赔时间期限延长到五月中旬。

7. Our cheque for USD4,000 was airmailed to you today in settlement of your claim for short weight of 550lbs.

今天航邮4 000美元支票一张，以偿付你方550磅的短重索赔。

8. We have received the 15 cases of Green Tea you sent us, but regret to say that on examination, five of them were found to be in a badly damaged condition. This was apparently attributable to faulty packing.

我方已收到你方运来的15箱绿茶，但遗憾的是，经检验，其中5箱损坏严重，很明显这是包装不良所致。

9. With mutual cooperation, this case has been settled amicably and we shall remit to you an amount of STG. 3,009 in compensation for the loss arising there from.

由于双方合作，此事已友好解决，我方将汇3 009英镑，赔偿你方损失。

10. Such case does exist but it counts for little. It is our hope that you will waive the claim and we shall see if we can do something for your orders which are to follow. 这样的事确实存在，但价值极微。我们希望你方撤回索赔，我方将会考虑对你方日后的订单给予适当优惠。

11. It would not be fair if the loss be totally imposed on us, as the liability rests with both parties. We are ready to pay 50% of the loss only.

责任应由双方承担，所有损失都加到我方头上是不公平的，我方只愿支付50％的损失。

12. We may compromise, but the compensation should, in no case, exceed STG. 300, otherwise, this case will be submitted to arbitration.

我方可以让步，但赔偿不得超过300英镑，否则将提交仲裁。

13. We regret our inability to accept your claim because the cases, when being loaded, left nothing to be desired.

歉难接受你方赔偿要求，因箱子在装船时，完整无损。

14. As it is a matter concerning the insurance, we hope that you will refer the claim to the insurance company or their agent at your end.

鉴于这是一个涉及保险的问题，希望你方向保险公司或其在贵地的代理人提出索赔。

15. Your claim for indemnity for the loss you sustained should, in our opinion, be referred to the shipping company, as the liability rests with them.

我方认为，由于责任在轮船公司，你方应向他们索赔遭受的损失。

16. We have to ask for compensation of GBP6,000 to cover the loss incurred as result of the inferior quality of the goods.

我们不得不向贵方索赔6 000英镑，作为因劣质货物给我方造成的损失赔偿。

17. If the buyer introduced by him fails to pay the principal or breaks the contract, it is the agent's responsibility to cover the loss.

如果他介绍的买方无力付款或撕毁合同，则由该代理商负责赔偿。

18. We have received your remittance in settlement of our claim.

我们已经收到你方解决我们索赔问题的汇款。

19. You should compensate us for the loss caused by the late delivery.

你方必须向我方赔偿因迟交货物所引起的损失。

20. So we consider that your claim for the loss to our company is not reasonable, and we can not accept, hope our explaination you can understand and support.

我们认为贵公司要我们索赔损失是不合理的，我们不接受索赔，希望我们的解释你们能够理解并给予支持。

练习题

1. 写作一封给卖方的投诉信，通知卖方9月7日装运的一批花瓶多数破损，经查明是由于包装不当所致，要求卖方退换受损货物。

2. 将下列内容译成英文

××先生:

8月1日第AG-3号合同下的小麦,定于10月底以前交货。作为签订合同的条件,你方保证提前交货,但至今尚未发运,对此我们甚感遗憾。

这样的交货拖延不是第一次了。鉴于一再发生迟交,我们不得不指出:在这种情况下,我们双方的业务往来恐怕难以长期持续下去。

切望上述情况能促使你公司设法最终解决按期交货问题。

3. 在已给出的单词中选择恰当的单词填入空内

**settlement   claim   claim   refer   with   to   to   to
alternative   compensation   by**

（1）We have been transacted _____ John Smith & Co . for more than 30 years.

（2）We should be pleased to finalize the first transaction with you but you should help us _____ bringing down your price.

（3）The inferior quality of your shipment causes us to lodge the _____ .

（4）As there is no direct sailing _____ your port, the shipment has to be delayed until next month.

（5）We cannot bear the responsibility for late delivery and you should submit your _____ to the shipping company.

（6）Our customers prefer Art, No.468 _____ Art, No.469 as the former is selling quickly here.

（7）Amicable _____ of a dispute is preferable to a law suit.

（8）We have no _____ but to ask for _____ to cover our loss.

（9）We regret that we cannot reach an agreement on our claim and therefore cannot but _____ the case to arbitration.

（10）Though the insurance is effected by us, please raise your claim to the PICC's agents at your end who will attend _____ the matter.

4. 结合如下情况写作一封处理买方索赔的信函

An American buyer has ordered 500 cases that you have had complaints from ZHEJIANG Tea Company. Upon arrival at New York port, 50 cases were found completely wet. The American buyer lodges a claim against this. In your reply, please include：

（1）a reasonable explanation about the case（s）to the damage;

（2）a solution to the buyer's claim. You may agree to settle the claim or refuse his request;

（3）use polite words to regain the buyer's lost confidence in you.

5. 将如下信函译成中文

Dear Sirs,

BA-8765-Wheat

We have received your letter of May 19, with enclosures, claiming for short weight and inferior quality on the consignment of Wheat shipped per S. S. "Prince"

We immediately looked into the matter and find that our wheat was properly weighed at the time of loading and the quality was up to standard. We, on our part, really cannot account for the reason of your complaint. But since the Wheat was examined by a public surveyor upon arrival at DALIAN, we cannot but accept your claims as tendered.

We therefore enclose our check No.2345 for US$ 25,000 in full and final settlement of your claims ABC-69 and 70. Please acknowledge receipt at your convenience.

We apologize for the trouble caused to you and would like to assure you that all possible steps will be taken by us to avoid any recurrence of similar nature in our future dealings with you.

Yours faithfully,

第十二章　代理

Agency

本章内容提要
本章内容包括建立代理关系和签定代理协议。

本章知识重点
如何撰写信函要求担任独家代理及对此类信函的回复，拟定和签定代理协议。

第一节 代理的写作要点
(Introduction on Agency)

一、对代理的介绍

国际贸易中相当数量的货物不是由买卖双方直接洽谈而成的，而是通过代理（通常在买方国境内）达成的。

代理是在国际贸易进出口业务中被习惯采用的一种做法。它是指委托人委托代理人作为其国外代表，并授权代理人为其在国外从事与贸易有关的各项活动，代理人和委托人的关系是委托代理关系。代理的种类很多，有销售代理（Selling agents）、购货代理（Buying agents）、运输代理（Forwarding agents）和信用担保代理（The del credere agents）等。

二、销售代理

销售代理是指在进出口业务中，委托人委托国外的代理在一定地区和一定时期内按照委托人的交易条件，借助代理人的经营能力、业务关系以及对当地市场的了解，来推销委托人的产品。销售代理选择的合适与否，对促进进出口和安全收回货款有着直接影响。因此，委托人应彻底调查候选代理对象的资格、经验及商业道德等情况，在签定代理协议（或合同）前确保：

1. 委托方能收回每一批货物的货款；

2. 代理方拥有为实现最高销售额所必需的高效的推销机构；

3. 代理方在其当地的客户和消费者中享有地位和信誉；

4. 代理方与其他商号没有任何可能妨碍委托人代理商品的业务关系。

如果调查结果满意，在签定代理协议（合同）时还需列入一些预防性条款，如规定一定期间的最低贸易额，或规定允许在发出短期的通知后终止合同。但在终止合同这一点上，应注意国外法律对通知的最短期限的规定。

独家代理是指在指定的地区内，由该独家代理人单独代表委托人行为，委托人不得在该地区再委托其他人作为代理。因此，独家代理是指委托人给予代理商在特定地区和一定期限内享有代销商品的专营权。通常，除非协议另有约定，一般也可允许委托人直接与指定的代理地区的买方进行交易。为了不损害独家代理的利益，有些协议规定，凡委托人直接与指定地区的买方达成交易的，仍然向独家代理计付佣金。

第二节　销售代理的范例讲解
（Sample Letters on Selling Agency）

一、申请代理的信函范例

Dear Sirs,

We understand from B&G Corporation that you are looking for a reliable firm with good connections in the cotton piece goods trade to represent you in Canada.

Having already had experience in marketing cotton piece goods similar to your own, we are familiar with customers' needs and are confident we could develop a worthwhile *market* for you in Canada. We have well-equipped showrooms in *Vancouver, Quebec* and an experienced sales staff who make regular calls on customers.

We should appreciate your letting us know as soon as possible whether you are interested in our offer and on what terms you would be willing to reach an agency agreement. *If it does*, we would suggest you meeting with Mr. Mark to discuss details of an agreement to both of us.

Yours faithfully,

(Signature)

General Manager

二、对申请代理的回复范例

Dear Sirs,

We thank you for your letter of November 16, in which you proposed to sell our products on agency basis.

We are deeply impressed by your kindness in submitting this proposal to us, and your application is now under our careful consideration. However, before going further into this arrangement, we would like to know your market consumption, the definite quantities you require quarterly or annually, your plan to push the sales of our products, your bank references, etc.

Last but not least, the whole matter ***hinges upon*** the question of the amount of commission you would require on orders obtained and executed. And as your Mr. Mark intends visiting Beijing at the end of November, we shall be pleased to discuss the possibility of coming to an agreement with him personally.

We are looking forward to your early reply and awaiting Mr. Mark's call.

Yours sincerely,

三、代理协议范本

Agency Agreement

This Agreement is ***entered into*** by and between the parties concerned on September 20, 2010 in Qingdao, China on the basis of equality and mutual benefit to develop business on terms and conditions mutually agreed upon as follow:

1. The Parties Concerned

Party A：Qingdao × × Industrial Co., Ltd.

Add: × × Road, Qingdao, China

E-mail:

Party B: × × Trading Company（Pte）Ltd.

Add: × × Street, Singapore

E-mail:

2. Appointment

Party A hereby appoints Party B as its Exclusive *Agent* to solicit orders for the commodity stipulated in Article 3 from customers in the *territory* stipulated in Article 4, and Party B accepts and assumes such appointment.

3. Commodity

" × × " brand washing machines

4. Territory

In Singapore only

5. Minimum turnover

Party B shall undertake to solicit orders for the above commodity from customers in the above territory during the effective period of this agreement for not less than USD 100, 000, 00.

6. Price and Payment

The price for each individual transaction shall be fixed through negotiations between Party B and the buyer, and subject to Party A's final confirmation.

Payment shall be made by confirmed, irrevocable L/C opened by the buyer in favor of Party A, which shall reach Party A 15 days before the date of shipment.

7. Exclusive Right

In consideration of the exclusive rights granted herein, Party A shall not, directly or indirectly, sell or export the commodity stipulated in Article 4 to customers in Singapore through channels other than Party B; Party B shall not sell, distribute or promote the sales of any products competitive with or similar to the above commodity in Singapore and shall not solicit or accept orders for the purpose of selling them outside Singapore. Party A shall refer to Party B any enquiries or orders for the commodity in question received by Party A from other firms in Singapore during the validity of this agreement.

8. Market Report

In order to keep Party A well informed of the prevailing market conditions, Party B should undertake to supply Party A, at least once a quarter or at any time when necessary, with market reports concerning changes of the local regulations in connection with the import and sales of the commodity covered by this agreement, local market tendency and the buyer's comments on quality, packing, price, etc. of the goods supplied by Party A under this agreement. Party B shall also supply party A with quotations and advertising materials on similar products of other suppliers.

9. Advertising and Expenses

Party B shall bear all expenses for advertising and publicity in connection with the commodity in question in Singapore within the validity of this agreement, and shall submit to Party A all audio and video materials intended for advertising for prior approval.

10. Commission

Party A shall pay Party B a commission of 5% on the net invoiced selling price on all orders directly obtained by Party B and accepted by party A. No commission shall be paid until Party A receives the full payment for each order.

11. Transactions between Governmental Bodies

Transactions between governmental bodies of Party A and Party B shall not be restricted by the terms and conditions of this agreement, nor shall the amount of such transactions be counted as part of the turnover stipulated in Article5.

12. Industrial Property Rights

Party B may use the trade-marks owned by Party A for the sale of the Washing Machines covered herein within the validity of this agreement, and shall acknowledge that all patents, trademarks, copy rights or any other industrial property rights used or embodied in the Washing Machines shall remain to be the sole properties of Party A. Should any infringement be found, Party B shall promptly notify and assist Party A to take steps to protect the latter's rights.

13. Validity of Agreement

This agreement, when duly signed by the both parties concerned, shall remain in force for 12 months from October 1, 2010 to September 30, 2011, and it shall be extended for another 12 months upon expiration unless notice in writing is given to the contrary.

14. Termination

During the validity of this agreement, if either of the two parties is found to have violated the stipulations herein, the other party has the right to terminate this agreement.

15. Force Majeure

Either party shall not be held responsible for failure or delay to perform all or any part of this agreement due to flood, fire, earthquake, draught, war or any other events which could not be predicted, controlled, avoided or overcome by the relative party. However, the party affected by the event of Force Majeure shall inform the other party of its occurrence in writing as soon as possible and thereafter send a certificate of the event issued by the relevant authorities to the other party within 15 days after its occurrence.

16. Arbitration

All disputes arising from the performance of this agreement shall be settled through friendly negotiation. Should no settlement be reached through negotiation, the case shall then be submitted for arbitration to the China International Economic and Trade Arbitration Commission（Beijing）and the rules of this commission shall be applied. The award of the arbitration shall be final and **binding** upon both parties.

Party A: Qingdao ××   Party B: ×× Trading

       Industrial Co., Ltd   Company（Pte），Ltd.

（Signature）   （Signature）

外贸代理协议范本（译文）

本协议于2010年9月20日在中国青岛由有关双方在平等互利的基础上达成，按双方同意的下列条件发展业务关系。

1. 协议双方

甲方：青岛××实业有限公司

地址：中国青岛××路××号

邮箱：

乙方：××贸易私人有限公司

地址：新加坡××街××号

邮箱：

2. 委任

甲方指定乙方为其独家代理，为第三条所列商品从第四条所列区域的顾客中招揽订单，乙方接受上述委任。

3. 代理商品

"××"牌洗衣机。

4. 代理区域

仅限于新加坡

5. 最低业务量

乙方同意，在本协议有效期内从上述代理区域内的顾客处招揽的上述商品的订单价值不低于10万美元。

6. 价格与支付

每一笔交易的货物价格应由乙方与买主通过谈判确定，并须经甲方最后确认。

付款使用保兑的、不可撤销的信用证，由买方开出，以甲方为受益人。信用证须在装运日期前15天到达甲方。

7. 独家代理权

基于本协议授予的独家代理权，甲方不得直接或间接地通过乙方以外的渠道向新加坡顾客销售或出口第三条所列商品，乙方不得在新加坡经销、分销或促销与上述商品相竞争或类似的产品，也不得招揽或接受以到新加坡以外地区销售为目的的订单，在本协议有效期内，甲方应将其收到的来自新加坡其他商家的有关代理产品的询价或订单转交给乙方。

8. 商情报告

为使甲方充分了解现行市场情况，乙方承担至少每季度一次或在必要时随时向甲方提供市场报告，内容包括与本协议代理商品的进口与销售有关的地方规章变动、当地市场发展趋势以及买方对甲方按协议供应的货物的品质、包装、价格等方面的意见。乙方还承担向甲方提供其他供应商类似商品的报价和广告资料。

9. 广告及费用

乙方负担本协议有效期内在新加坡销售代理商品做广告宣传的一切费用，并向甲方提交所用于广告的声像资料，供甲方事先核准。

10. 佣金

对乙方直接获取并经甲方确认接受的订单，甲方按净发票售价向乙方支付5%的佣金。佣金在甲方收到每笔订单的全部货款后才会支付。

11. 政府部门间的交易

在甲、乙双方政府部门之间达成的交易不受本协议条款的限制，此类交易的金额也不应计入第五条规定的最低业务量。

12. 工业产权

在本协议有效期内，为销售有关洗衣机，乙方可以使用甲方拥有的商标，并承认使用于或包含于洗衣机中的任何专利商标、版权或其他工业产权为甲方独家拥有。 一旦发现侵权，乙方应立即通知甲方并协助甲方采取措施保护甲方权益。

13. 协议有效期

本协议经有关双方如期签署后生效，有效期为1年，从2010年10月1日至2011年9月30日。除非做出相反通知，本协议期满后将延长12个月。

14. 协议的终止

在本协议有效期内，如果一方被发现违背协议条款，另一方有权终止协议。

15. 不可抗力

由于水灾、火灾、地震、干旱、战争或协议一方无法预见、控制、避免和克服的其他事件导致不能或暂时不能全部或部分履行本协议，该方不负责任。但是，受不可抗力事件影响的一方须尽快将发生的事件通知另一方，并在不可抗力事件发生15天内将有关机构出具的不可抗力事件的证明寄交对方。

16. 仲裁

因履行本协议所发生的一切争议应通过友好协商解决。如协商不能解决争议，则应将争议提交中国国际经济贸易仲裁委员会（北京），依据其仲裁规则进行仲裁。仲裁裁决是终局的，对双方都有约束力。

甲方：青岛××实业限公司　　　乙方：××贸易私人有限公司

　　（签字）　　　　　　　　　　　　（签字）

四、重要词句

1. market n. 市场，销路

　　a promising market 有销路的市场

　　lose one's market 失去买卖机会

market uncertain 市场状况不定

market glutted 市场饱和

overrun one's market 不肯脱手以致失去出售机会

market v. 营销=to sell products in an organized way and on a large scale

in the market for sth. =want to buy sth. 想购买某物

2. Vancouver 温哥华

Vancouver is the chief Pacific port of Canada in British Columbia having prosperous trade relations with China. The city is also a center of Chinese immigrants in that country.

温哥华是加拿大的一个主要的太平洋港口，位于大不列颠哥伦比亚省，与中国有着繁荣的贸易往来。温哥华同时也是一个中国移民聚集的城市。

3. Quebec 魁北克

加拿大东部之一省，首府与省同名，该省为法语区，法裔居民占80％以上。

4. If it does "如果这样的话

5. last but not least=equally important最后但同样重要的，是英语中的一个常用短语

6. hinge upon=depend on以……而定，介词upon也可以换做on, 文内译为"关键在……"

e.g. The development of the negotiation hinges on both parties' attitudes.

谈判的进展取决于双方的态度。

China's future economic growth will, to a large extent, hinge upon boosting domestic demand, and investment increase will have an important role to play.

未来中国经济增长很大程度上取决于扩大内需，投资的增加将扮演重要角色。

7. agency n.代理，代理业务，代理处

e.g. The agency is granted and accepted by the Principal.

代理业务由委托人授予并认可。

8. enter into...本义为"参加"、"开始"此处译为"签订"。

e.g. A US importer entered into a contract directly with a manufacturer in Guangdong.

一个美国进口商直接与广东的一家制造公司签订了合同。

We are willing to enter into business relations with your firm on the basis of equality and mutual benefit.

我们愿在平等互利、互通有无的基础上与你公司建立业务关系。

9. agent n. 代理人，代理，代理公司

e.g. The principal shall terminate the agency by... days' written notice to the agent.

委托人可以用为期……天的书面通知告知代理人终止代理业务。

When opportunity matures, we will appoint you（as）our exclusive agent for the USA.

当机会成熟时，我们将委托你为我方在美国的独家代理。

10. territory n. 商业上推销、代理的业务区域范围

e.g. The territory covered by this agreement is confined to Guangdong.

本协议规定的代理区域为广东省。

11. bind v. bound（p.p）（受……的约束）

e.g. This agreement shall bind each party and its assignees.

本协议对签署各方和受让人具有约束力。

A company should be bound by its articles of association.

一家公司应该受它自己章程的约束。

第三节　代理协议书的实用例句
（Useful Sentences on Agency Agreement）

一、申请成为代理的实用例句

1. We are venturing to request you to appoint us as your agent in China for your textiles.

我们冒昧地要求你方委托我方为你方纺织品在中国的代理。

2. We wish to handle as an exclusive agent in this line.

我们希望以独家代理的方式经营这一行业。

3. Since we have dealt in recorders for more than 40 years, we believe that we can offer expertise in obtaining orders and handling sales in this line.

由于我们经营录音机已经有40多年了，我们相信在获得订单和处理此类商品的销售方面有专长。

4. Having a wide and varied experience in the trade, we are convince that we are in a position to take care of your import business as a buying agent in the most effective manner.

我们有着广泛的、多方面的贸易经验，确信能最有效地担负起作为贵公司进口代理的责任。

5. We should be glad if you would consider our application to act as your agency for the sale of your shoes.

如能考虑我们担任贵公司鞋类销售代理的申请，我们会很高兴。

6. Is it possible to increase the commission to 4%?

能不能把佣金提高到4%呢?

二、同意指定代理或商谈代理的实用例句

1. After investigation and due consideration, we have decided to appoint you our agent in the district you defined, subject to the following terms and conditions.

经过调查和适当考虑，我们决定按照下列条件，在贵方提出的地区内由贵方担任我方代理。

2. We are pleased to confirm the agency agreement reached during our discussion last month and are looking forward to a happy and successful working relationship with you.

我方现欣然确认我们上个月磋商达成的代理协议，并期望和贵方享有愉快和成功的工作关系。

3. We have noted your request for acting as our agent in your area, but before going further into the matter, we would like to know your plan for promoting the sales and the annual turnover you may realize in your market.

我方已注意到贵公司的要求，在贵地区作为我方代理。但在洽谈此事之前，我方想了解贵方的推销计划和在贵地区市场的可能实现的年销量。

4. As the returns from your present turnover are insufficient to cover our rising costs, we are afraid that the business between us cannot be continued except on a higher level of sales.

由于从你们目前营业额获得的利润不足以支付日益增加的费用。因此，除非有一个较高销售水平；否则，恐怕我们之间的业务不能继续下去了。

5. As regards the question of sole agency, in our opinion, we both had better leave it in abeyance pending the development of business.

关于独家代理问题，我们的意见是，双方暂且不谈，留待交易发展后再说。

6. Our agents in other areas usually get a 3%~5% commission.

我方其他地区的代理通常得到3%~5%的佣金。

练习题

1. 用合适的词语填空

（1）We are seeking a reliable representative who terms you would undertake to buy _____ us _____ commission.

（2）The salary as agreed _____ the contract will be transferred monthly to the representative's account.

（3）We are offering a general agency _____ our textiles in Canada. How about you?

（4）We are already represented by our _____ agent in your city for the _____ of our Enamelware.

（5）For ... we are looking for a young man to act _____ our connections.

2. 翻译如下语句

（1）我们对贵方提出作为我方棉质衬衣料的独家代理一事，深表谢意。由于彼此尚不熟悉，我们认为待达成一些实际交易之后再来考虑此事较为妥当。

（2）很对不起，我们不得不谢绝贵方关于担任我方代理人的申请，因为此方面的业务已由贵市的××公司按独家经营条件经营。

（3）代理问题尚在考虑中，诚盼在现阶段继续努力推销我们的产品。

（4）考虑到你公司在推销雨伞方面的经验，贵方市场又有潜力，我们决定委托贵公司为我们在贵国市场的独家代理。

（5）We are very glad to learn from your letter of July 7 that you are willing to accept an agency for marketing our products in UK.

（6）There should be no sales of competing products to be made in your country either on your own account or account of any other firm or company.

（7）A commission of 5%, based on FOB values of all goods shipped to UK, whether on orders placed through you or not, payable at the end of each quarterly period.

（8）We accept your terms and conditions set out in the draft agency agreement and look forward to a happy and successful working relationship with you.

3. 翻译如下信函

Letter 1

Dear Sir,

We thank you for your letter of 14th September.

As we are now only at the get-acquainted stage we deem that it rather premature to take into consideration the matter of sole agency. In our opinion, it would be better for both of us to try out a period of cooperation to see how things prove. Also, it would be necessary for you to test the marketability of our products at your end and to continue your efforts in building a larger turnover to justify the sole agency arrangement.

We enclose two copies of our latest pricelist covering all the products we handle within the framework of your specialized lines.

We shall be pleased to hear from you again.

Yours faithfully,

Letter 2

执事先生：

我参加了最近召开的广州秋季交易会，对你方手表的上乘质量、合理设计和具有竞争力的价格印象深刻。我们深信开罗对你方产品有着广阔的市场。如果你们在这里没有代理，我们有意做你方的代理。

我们是在手表贸易方面已有20多年经验的进口商和经销商，对市场了如指掌，而且与主要零售商有着良好的联系。我们坚信，为在开罗销售你方产品而设代理对我们双方都有好处。

敬候佳音。

第十三章　商务传真与电子邮件

Fax and E-mail

本章内容提要
本章内容包括商务传真与电子邮件的格式和写作要求。

本章知识重点
如何撰写商务传真和电子邮件，重点掌握电子邮件写作的注意事项。

第一节　商务传真与电子邮件的写作要点
（Introduction on Fax and E-mail）

一、商务传真写作要点

Fax是Facsimile的缩写，是一种非常现代化的通信方式，是目前商务活动中使用较为广泛的沟通工具之一。大部分的公司、企业和机构，甚至一些家庭都安装了传真机，其操作简单方便。商务传真的格式非常简单，所包含的信息也与信函基本一样。商务传真的优势有以下几点。

1. 沟通迅捷，等同于国际长途。

2. 费用低廉，远低于国际长途。

3. 可以完整再现图案、表格和签名等。

4. 24小时服务，可随时接收信息。

商务传真由三部分构成：第一部分是题头，内容包括收、发传真双方的基本情况，先写收件人（To）的情况，再写发件人（From）以及发送传真的日期与传真页数；第二部分为主题与正文；第三部分为结尾。

为了方便收件人阅读、辨认以及公司内部保存文件，很多公司都规定了自己的传真页面格式。首先在信头下加印或键入标题"传真"或"传真封面"，然后详细列出以下信息：发件人和收件人的名称、电话和传真号，发函日期，页数等。

在写作传真的过程中应避免使用很粗的字体或多种不同颜色的字体，只有简洁明了的字体才能使发出的传真清晰可辨；还应避免出现大面积色彩浓重的段落，这将会导致传输过程加长，让收件人在接收传真时承担更多的油墨费，或长时间地占用传真机；还要尽量避免加注脚，由于注脚字体偏小，容易导致接收时无法辨认。

一般情况下，公司有专门的传真用纸，上面已印上了公司的地址、电话和传真号，发送人只要填好日期、对方电话和传真号即可。

二、电子邮件写作要点

由于电子邮件既具备传真的优点，又有着成本更低、操作更简便的特点，所以使用越来越普遍。据调查，约有88％的互联网用户使用电子邮件，而在商务领域中约有90％的员工通过电子邮件的形式来联系公务。所以，电子邮件的写作在业务往来中占据着举足轻重的地位。业务往来电子邮件代表着公司的形象，显示着公司的水平和实力，直接影响到客户对公司的评价。提高电子邮件的写作质量可以减少误解、提高沟通效率。本节将重点介绍商务英语电子邮件的格式、写作原则及注意事项。

1. 商务英语电子邮件的格式

常见的商务英语电子邮件由如下五部分构成。

（1）From: 写信人电子邮件地址

To：收信人电子邮件地址

C.C.：抄送收信人电子邮件地址

B.C.C.：密送收信人电子邮件地址（抄送信息却不被其他人知道）

（2）Subject: 主题摘要

-URGENT-急件标示方法

（3）Salutation: 称呼

Beginning: 开头

Body: 正文，内容通常包括写作的原因，要求对方采取的行动等

Ending: 结尾

（4）Complimentary close：结尾敬语

（5）Writer's full name:写信人全名

Writer's title and department: 写信人职务及所属部门

Other information may include company's name, logo, address, phone number, fax number and website:其他信息，包括公司名称、标识、地址、电话号码、传真号码和网址

下面详细介绍各个构成部分的写作要点。

（1）邮件的写信人电子邮件地址、收信人电子邮件地址、抄送收信人电子邮件地址以及密送收信人电子邮件地址这四部分的处理比一般信件要简单得多，无需填写繁杂的邮政地址，只需填入相应的电子邮件地址即可，而且并非每一项都填，若收信人只有一个，就不需填写抄送收信人电子邮件地址。

（2）若知道对方姓和名却无法识别对方的性别时，不应乱猜测对方的性别，可用Dear+ First name+ Surname作为称呼，如Dear Imran Jawed或Dear Moira Gedding。

（3）主题摘要：邮件的标题应当意思明确、信息具体化。邮件标题是邮件主要内容的浓缩，也是读者浏览信箱时决定是否读邮件的依据。邮件标题选择合适与否也影响读者处理信箱中信件的效率。因此，为了确保收信人及时阅读邮件，邮件的标题不仅要引人注目，而且应该意思明确，避免模糊笼统。此外，发信人还应注意标题为名词短语或动名词短语。如下例：

a. This is very important! Read Immediately!

b. meeting!

c. questions about Meeting!

d. on the Sales Meetings!

以上四个标题中，a项既不是名词短语，也没有体现邮件的主旨，b和c过于笼统，只有d项最为妥当，信息明确、一目了然。

（4）称呼：邮件开头的称呼语应礼貌得体，符合商务英语的写作习惯。使用称呼语的一般原则是：① 下属写给上司或双方关系较为正式时一般用Dear Mr./Mrs./Miss/Ms.+ surname（姓）作为称呼，如Dear Mr. Jackson, Dear Mrs. Anniston, Dear Miss Jones。其中Mrs.用于已婚妇女，Miss用于未婚女子，Ms.作为未知婚否女子的礼节尊称，相当于中文里的"女士"。② 若不知道对方的姓名但知道对方的商务头衔，可用Dear+ Title作为称呼，如Dear Credit Manager, Dear Sales Manager, Dear Human Resources Manager，这些称呼比Dear Sir or Madam要更清楚、更可取。

（5）若邮件是一封通函，同时群发给几个人收时，可用Dear all作为邮件称呼。

（6）若双方关系较亲近，可用Dear+ First name或Hi+ First Name作为称呼，后者在美国英语中尤为盛行，如Dear Thomas、Hi Ben等。需要注意的是称呼后面一定要用逗号，称呼应自成一行，与邮件的正文隔开。美国、加拿大等国的正式商务电子邮件中，还可能会用冒号，如"Dear Mr. Jones:"。

（7）开头：万事开头难，商务邮件更是如此，因此有必要掌握邮件开头的写作规律及实用句型。邮件的开头因邮件内容的不同而有所变化，但无论何种商务邮件，开头一般都需表明写信的缘由或主旨，常见的开头句型如下。

a. I am writing because/to...

b. I am writing in connection with...

c. On Saturday, 3rd March, I bought a BX Mountain bike from your shop. Since then I have had to return it eight times for repairs.

d. The noise made by the work-men in your apartment is causing me considerable discomfort.

若是回函或写信前与收信人已经联系过（例如通过电话等），开头应提到对方的邮件或提及这一联系，常见的开头句型如下。

e. Thank you for your E-mail of 12th May in which you asked for information about holidays in Thailand.

f. Further to our meeting last Tuesday, I am sending you the amendments to the contract as we agreed.

（8）正文：正文是邮件的主体，是最重要的部分。这一部分的写作好坏决定了整篇邮件的水平和质量。写作时应牢记"5C"原则。此外，正文写好之后应进行编排，确保其结构清晰，便于读者阅读。如正文内容较长，可使用小标题、小段落，或利用星号、下划线及段落间空行等方式使邮件条理清楚、一目了然。正文中需要注意的问题列示如下。

a. 使用小段落，尽量做到每个小话题都用一个段落来阐述。

b. 段落与段落之间空一行。

c. 提供段落的小标题。

d. 使用列举符号罗列具体信息。

e. 使用项目符号或下划线强调重点内容。

详见下例。

Dear Mr. White,

Further to our telephone conversation yesterday, we would like to confirm your additional requests and are pleased to provide the following services for you.

- Provide two rooms from March 15th to the 17th.

- Provide ten tables for each room.

- Provide a TV and DVD in one room.

- Serve lunch on the 16th.

We guarantee that you will enjoy our excellent service. If you have any other questions, please feel free to contact us. We are looking forward to meeting you soon.

Sincerely,

Bush Jackson

Officer Arrowhead Conference Center

（9）结尾：邮件的结尾部分一般指明写信人将采取的行动或写信人希望收信人采取某种行动或反应。这部分应避免画蛇添足，造成累赘感；同时也应注意措辞礼貌得体，语调积极乐观，给收信人留下良好的印象。常见句型如下。

a. I am looking forward to meeting you soon.

b. Thank you for your cooperation. We wish to take you as our regular customer.

c. I would appreciate it if you could confirm the order by the end of this month.

d. If you require further copies of the contract, please contact me and I will arrange for them to be sent to you.

（10）结尾敬语：一般信函的结尾敬语有几种，在英国Yours faithfully是正规用法，在美国常用Sincerely yours，这两种作为电子邮件的结尾敬语都略显冗长而老套。一般来说，正式的邮件可用Sincerely，若双方比较熟悉、亲近时，可用Regards。注意结尾敬语的第一个词的头一个字母要大写，敬语后面要加逗号。

（11）写信人全名：在结尾敬语空一行处，写信人应该写上自己的名和姓。若读者是关系比较亲近的同事或商业伙伴，可不加姓。中国人的姓名就按照汉语拼音写，姓和名的第一字母都要大写。若是双名，其汉语拼音应作为一个整体，不能分开，而且第一字母需大写。此外，写信人应注意的是无需将姓和名颠倒，如：Zhang Zihua是正确的写法，而ZihuaZhang、Zhang Zi Hua则不妥。

（12）写信人职务及所属部门：增加这部分信息主要是为了便于收信人了解写信人的身份，以便在回邮件的时候采取恰当的称呼和写作语气。

（13）其他信息：这部分可能包括写信人公司的名称、标志、地址、电话号码、传真号码和网址等。

2. 商务英语电子邮件写作应遵循的5C原则

（1）准确原则（Correctness）

由于商务英语电子邮件涉及商务活动双方的权利、义务关系，其准确性对商务治理与沟通至关重要。具体而言，不仅电子邮件的英语语法、标点符号和拼写要做到准确无误，电子邮件的内容还要叙述准确，不要说过头，也不宜漏说略述。此外，还应避免使用一些语意模糊的词语或短语，如：Majority、ASAP等，以免引起不必要的纠纷。

（2）简洁原则（Conciseness）

简洁原则是商务英语写作最重要的原则，指在不影响完整性和礼貌性的前提下，尽量使用简单句子和简短词语。一封拖沓冗长、措辞复杂的电子邮件既浪费写作时间，也会给阅读者带来不必要的麻烦，故商务英语电子邮件应以简明扼要为第一要务，写信人应尽可能用简洁的文字完整、清楚地表达意思。

另外，为了节约时间和空间，电子邮件中有时可使用约定俗成的缩略语，如Info表示information，Qty表示quantity，PC表示piece，L/C表示Letter of Credit，FOB表示Free on Board。

例1. It is very difficult to sell manhole covers in France. This product must have the quality certificate issued in France.

例2. Price：USD 96/PC FOB Shanghai.

例3. Hope you can accept it.

例1中的两个单句具有明显的因果关系，但是并不使用表达因果关系的连接词如since、because，这种舍长句、复合句，选短句、简单句，喜并列、弃从属的句法特征在商务英语电子邮件写作中十分常见。例2中缩略语的使用，例3中不完整句的选择反映出与普通商务信函相比，商务电子邮件更倾向于非正式文体，更为口语化。

（3）清楚原则（Clarity）

商务英语电子邮件要写得清楚、明白、毫无晦涩难懂之处，使收信人看了信后不会误解写信人的意图；要尽量做到开门见山、直入正题；要做到层次清楚、用词准确。

例1. We will deliver your goods soon.

例1中soon表示不久、很快，语义不明确，没有指出具体的供货时间，可改为具体的日期。

（4）完整原则（Complete）

商务电子邮件的内容应力求具体、明确、完整，提供读者所需要的信息，尤其像询问贸易条件等需要回函的电子邮件，更需要清楚完整地表达意思，因为只有包含具体信息的邮件才能达到良好的沟通效果。邮件是否完整，可以用5W1H原则来检验，即Who，When，Where，What，Why和How。

（5）礼貌原则（Courtesy）

商务英语电子邮件应遵循措辞婉转、礼貌的原则。电子邮件有时直接影响到整个交易的成败，买卖双方应十分注重措辞方式，语气要真诚、善解人意、考虑周全，使对方容易接受，而不要盛气凌人。在写作电子邮件时，可以通过使用虚拟语气、委婉语气等方法迂回地表达观点，提出要求，避免使用冒犯、伤害、贬低的短语，如"Your neglectful attitude"、"impatience"、"We deny your claim"等；为了做到礼貌得体，应多使用诸如"please，your kind inquiry"、"I would appreciate it if you would..."等词语和句式。

例1. If it is not for the larger orders we receive from a number of our regular customers，we could not have quoted for supplies even at that price.

例2. I would appreciate it if you could give me your best quotations for 65,000 pieces.

例1中虚拟语气和例2中委婉语气的使用，缓和了商务谈判的语气，既明确了自己的立场，又使对方的面子免于受损，语气自然诚恳、礼貌得体，很容易为对方所接受。

3. 商务英语电子邮件写作的其他注意事项

和一般商务信函相比，商务电子邮件除了有自己的习惯格式以外，最大的特点是通过互联网这一媒介，其传送的速度比一般信函要快，也正是因为这一特点才使其受到越来越多商务人士人的青睐。然而，人们在享受这一快捷服务的同时，也应根据网络的特征注意以下几点。

（1）了解收信人和抄送收信人的区别。一般来说，写信人不会期望被抄送的收信人回复或采取某种行动。

（2）选择一个职业化的邮箱地址。诸如SexyGirl、CoolCat、Smallfish等邮箱名称显得过于随意，不适于正式商务沟通，有些公司对此甚至有专门的规定。

（3）不要发送对方不需要的邮件（即垃圾邮件），特别是随意抄送，以免浪费对方的宝贵时间。

（4）邮件若携带附件，应在邮件中加以说明。传递附件时，应当注意尽量减少附件的数量；若附件容量较大，还应对其进行压缩，从而缩短收件人的下载时间。

（5）写邮件时应心平气和，切莫在生气时发邮件，以免写出一些对商务沟通不利的言语。

（6）避免过度使用缩略语。诸如"Immed，IOW，RGDS，FYR，FTF"等常用于网络聊天的缩略语或手机短信语言，不宜用在商务邮件中。它们相应的正确写法为"Immediately，In other words，Regards，For your reference，Face to face，Thanks"。当然，类似于"Mr，Mrs."等缩略语早已成为正式的表达，如用完整的拼写反而不妥。

（7）一般邮件中都自动生成写信日期。若要加日期，可以放在邮件的底部，但写法要规范。

（8）在点击"Send（发送）"之前，应当仔细阅读邮件，以确保信息、语法及拼写正确。一封含有语法错误的邮件会有损公司的形象，也会令人费解；一封邮件若出现信息错误，轻则导致沟通失败，重则会带来经济损失。

随着国际商务活动的不断扩展，商务英语电子邮件的重要性也日益明显。同时，电子商务的普及也会让邮件的作者忽视商务英语电子邮件应有的规范和格式，难免会出现这样或那样的问题。而准确、规范的英文邮件，不仅能反应写信人的英语及业务水平，还可以体现写信人为人处事的态度和风格，有助于建立良好的商务关系，最终对达成贸易起到重要的作用。因此，有必要熟悉商务英文电子邮件应有的规范和格式，遵循邮件的写作原则。

第二节　商务传真与电子邮件的范例讲解
（Samples of Fax and E-mail）

一、商务传真范例

范例1

CRYSTAL LOGISTICS LTD

Vicarage Drive, Barking, Essex 1g117NA

Telephone: 081-5513 2235　Fax: 081-5513 2221

No. of Pages：2

To: Mr. Zhang Yueyi　　　　　　　　　　Fax: 0086 21 6595 8000

COSCO SHANGHAI INT'L FREIGHT CO.LTD

From: John Smith

CRYSTAL LOGISTICS LTD

Date: 3rd March 2010

C.C.: Sue Prazer

EXEL LOGISTICS

Dear Mr. Zhang,

RE: ZHONG HE V. 0063E. TRIU 9551882 5c/s 917kg7.57m3；YUNHE V.0030E, CBHU9733042, 2c/s853kg5.91m3

The above-mentioned shipments have been loaded onto *COSCO* regular service and are bound for Qingdao port via Shanghai. Crystal Logistics have notified you that we pay for the *T/S fee + on carriage* charge to Qingdao.

This morning I received a phone call form the shipper who has expressed dissatisfaction with our service. Apparently the British consulate has been in contact with your goods shipper about the ***transshipment formalities***. They have told the shipper in the U.K. that the goods must move under Bond（for which they have to pay $1,500 USD）to Qingdao. Since the shipper has paid the on-carriage to Qingdao to Crystal Logistics, COSCO Freight Shanghai must take this cargo, after ***clearing*** at Shanghai, to Qingdao ***CFS***.

Please advise us if there are any problems with the usual method of shipping to Qingdao.

Best Regards

John Smith

范例2：

Herbert Import & Export	何伯特进出口公司
Telephone:（212）2215608	电话:（212）2215608
Fax:（123）555-5436	传真:（212）2215706
388 Station Street , New York ,10018 U.S.A.	美国纽约车站街388号10018
FACSIMILE TRANSMISSION	传真发送给:
To: × × Company	× ×公司
Date: May 23,2010	日期:2010年5月23日
Attn: Eric Lee	收件人:埃里克·李
From: Simon Davis	发件人:西蒙·戴维斯
Your Ref.:2051/ef	贵方编号:2051/ef
Our Ref.:5237/nl	我方编号:5237/nl
C.C.:Kate Long	抄送:凯特·郎
Page:1	页数:1

Dear Sirs:

　　We are an American company, our shares are ***to be issued*** next month. Our company is to be granted a bank credit soon. Should you be interested in cooperation or in buying our shares, please do not hesitate to contact us. We look forward to hearing from you .

Yours Sincerely,

Simon Davis

Managing Director

二、电子邮件范例

范例 1

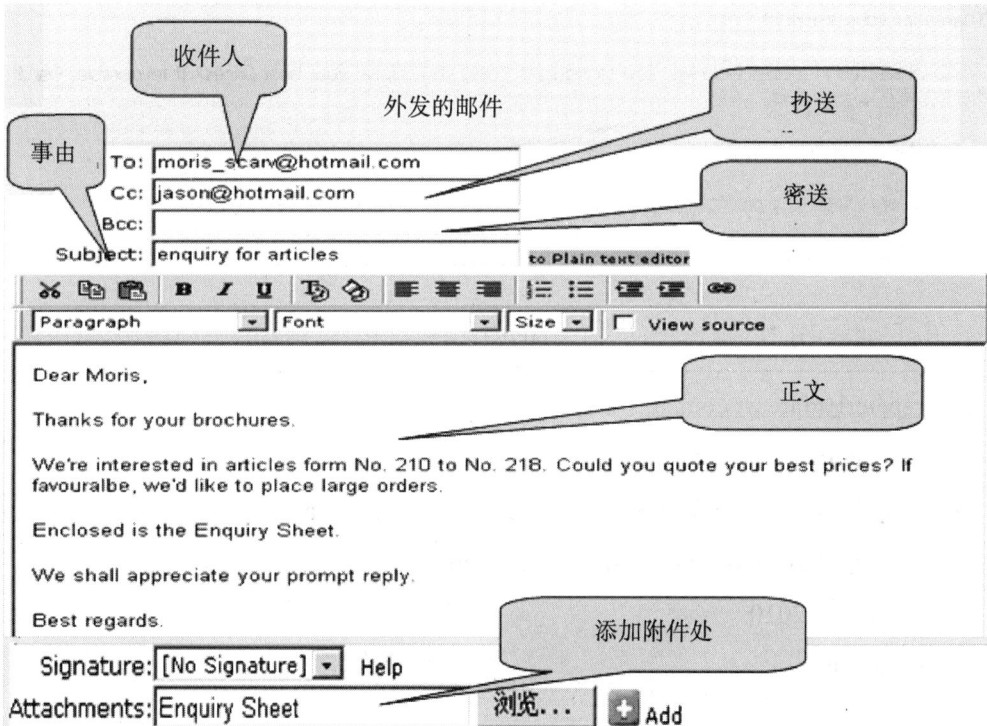

范例 2

接收的邮件

发件人

收件人　事由

抄送人

日期

附件

From : jackywang < jackywang@ziplip.com>
Reply-To : jackywang < jackywang@ziplip.com>
To : Moris_scarv@hotmail.com
CC : jason@hotmail.com
Subject : enquiry for articles
Date : Fri, 29 Nov 2002 00:01:45 -0800 (PST)
Attachment : EnquirySheet.xls (32k)

Reply　Reply All　Forward　Delete　Put in Folder...　▼　**Printer Friendly Version**

Dear Moris,

Thanks for your brochure.

We're interested in articles from No. 210 to No.218. Could you quote your best prices? If favourable, we'd like to place large orders.

Enclosed is the Enquiry Sheet.

We shall appreciate your prompt reply.

正文

Best regards.

范例 3

To: sspeterl@fareast.com.sg（Service Section）

From: ssdonh@fareast.com.sg（Service Section）

Subject: Air-conditioning system for the freight transfer area

C.C.: psmarthal@fareast.com.sg（Purchasing Section）

Date: 26 May 2010

Attachments:

Hi Peter,

As you know, we now have approval to purchase a new air-conditioning system for the freight transfer area.

I would like you to approach the following three companies ***with a view to*** obtaining the technical specifications and quotations for air-conditioning systems suitable for our needs. We require a system which will serve an area of 15,000 sq feet. Could you also ensure that the systems that you investigate have a ***long guarantee*** and that regular ***maintenance*** visits are part of the agreement?

The three companies are:

. Yang Fat Air Condition Co.（Tel: 65 545 5643/ Fax: 65 654 8765）

. Tramin（Tel: 65 552 6321/ Fax: 65 553 8977）

. Mega Air Conditioning（Tel: 65 621 9097/ Fax: 65 655 4562）

Lastly, can you please tell them that we need the system installed by mid-June at the latest?

Thanks.

Don Howard

范例4

To: Symonds@yahoo.com

Date: 26th December2010 10:30 pm

Subject: Establishment of Business Relations

Enclosure: Price List & Order

Dear Mr. Pollock,

We are one of the leading exporters of Chinese Silk goods and in this line for over 30 years. We believe you will be quite satisfied with our services and the excellent quality of our goods.

Enclosed please find the latest price list of our goods and a copy of our order.

We are looking forward to your favorable reply.

Best regards,

Wang Qiang

三、重要词句

1. COSCO: China Ocean Shipping（Group）Company 中国远洋运输（集团）公司

2. T/S fee: transshipment fee 中转费

3. on-carriage 货运中转

On-carriage-Transport from the port of arrival in the country of destination to the buyer's premises, usually by truck, rail or inland waterways.

货运中转——从目的国的到达港到买方地点的运输，通常通过卡车、铁路或内河水路进行运输。

4. transshipment formality 转船手续

5. clearing 清关

6. CFS: container freight station 集装箱货运站

7. to be issued 将要发行，这种结构表示一种按照计划或安排即将发生的动作或作为

8. with view to doing sth 为……起见，为的是做……

9. long guarantee 长期保修

10. maintenance n.保持,维护

11. Our shares are to be issued next month. 我们的股票将于下个月发行。

Our company is to be granted a World Bank credit soon.我们公司即将获得一笔世界银行贷款。

这种结构还用来表示如下几种意思。

（1）可能发生的行为，如下例。

The credit is to be granted when we have enough money。我们有了一定资金后即可获得贷款。

（2）注定要发生的行为，如下例。

All supplies are to written in our records。所有供货我们都记录在案。

这种结构除了用被动语态外，也可以用主动语态，如下例。

The Board are to meet tomorrow。董事会将于明天召开。

当并列句用这种结构时，并列连词及动词"be"均可省略，如下例。

e.g. We are a company in the course of privatization，our shares to be issued next month。

我方为一家正在向私有化转制的公司，我方股票将于下个月发行。

上述例句加上并列连词和动词"be"后是这样的：

We are a company in the course of privatization and our shares are to be issued next month.

e.g. We want to discuss the terms of the contract，our company to be granted a World Bank credit soon。

我们想讨论一下合同条款，因我们公司将很快得到一笔世界银行贷款。

上句如果补充完整应是这样的：

We want to discuss the terms of the contract as our company is to be granted a World Bank credit soon.

第三节　商务传真与电子邮件的实用例句
（Useful Sentences on Fax and E-mail）

以下是一些关于商务传真与电子邮件的典型例句。

1. Replying to your fax enquiry, we're pleased to E-mail you an information pack which includes all the details of our service.

回复你方传真咨询，我们将会电邮一份详细介绍我们业务范围的信息包给你们。

2. Could you give us some idea about your price?

请介绍贵方的价格好吗？

3. Let's meet each other halfway.

我们各让一半。

4. I'm attaching an order.

兹附上订单一份。

5. Following your yesterday's E-mail/fax instructions, we have today sent the

subject order to you.

按你方昨天的电子邮件/传真要求，我方已于今日将标题项下订货发出。

6. Hopefully, I'll be able to place an order if the queries are satisfactorily answered.

疑虑如能得到圆满解答，我将有望下订单。

7. Unless otherwise stated or agreed upon, all prices are net without commission.

除非另有规定或经双方同意，所有价格都是不含佣金的净价。

8. We strongly advise you to accept the offer as our stocks are running low.

我方力荐贵方接受报盘，因为我们的存货很快告罄。

9. If you find our offer acceptable. Please fax us for confirmation.

如贵公司接受上述报价，请传真落实订单。

练习题

1. 将如下商务传真译成英文并添加传真题头

尊敬的瑞德先生：

感谢您2010年8月18日的来信，您信中提出演示我方产品SJX34型的要求，我已安排我方代表于2010年9月10日下午2点去您处做产品演示。同时，若需详情，请与我联系。

此致

2. 阅读如下电子邮件并译成中文

To: gloriac@siufat.com.hk（Purchasing）

From: stfrankp@siufat.com.hk（Stores）

Subject: Low oil heater stock level ZAZQ`

C.C.

Date: 16 May, 2010

Attachments:

Hi, Gloria,

You may remember that at the end of October I sent you a message reminding you that we urgently needed to increase our stock of oil heaters for the coming cold season.

I have recently noticed that our stock of oil heaters is dangerously low, and that unless we order a large number in the very near future, the store will run out in the middle of our heavy period.

We urgently need at least 150 Cosyheat Model CS15 oil heaters and 200 CS18 oil heaters if we are to meet demand. Please order these as soon as possible from the manufactures.

Best wishes,

3. 将如下内容，译成中文电子邮件并添加发信人，收信人、时间和邮箱地址

非常高兴收到贵方9月19日电邮。

对贵方打算与我方建立直接业务关系一事，我方很感兴趣。这恰好也是我方的愿望。我方一贯坚持在平等互利的基础上与国外企业或公司共同合作，以促进我们业务和关系的发展。现附上我方经营的项目及产品目录供贵方参考。期盼收到您的早日回复。

第十四章　其他商务文书

Other Business Documents

本章内容提要

本章内容包括公司内部的一些常见商务文书，如备忘录及会议记录。

本章知识重点

了解如何撰写备忘录及会议记录，掌握信函与其他商务文书写作的区别。

第一节　备忘录及会议记录的写作要点
（Introduction on Memo and Minutes of Meeting）

一、备忘录写作要点

备忘录（Memorandum）是商务文书中的一种，主要用于公司内部职员、部门间通报信息，如会议安排、情况报告、问题处理等，在英语中称为interoffice memorandum，其复数为memoranda，简称memo。除了可以采用纸质信函形式之外，备忘录也可以通过电子邮件发出。

备忘录有约定俗成的结构和格式，一般包含以下六个部分。

■ 标题（Memo/MEMO）

■ 收件人（To）：……

■ 发件人（From）：……

■ 发文日期（Date）：……

■ 事由（Subject）：……

■ 正文（Message）

1. 标题

在备忘录中，必须要使用一个标题，例如"MEMO"，或者"INTEROFFICE CORRESPONDENCE"。标题全部用大写，在页面居中或左对齐。

2. 收件人、发件人、发文日期

在备忘录的顶端要加上一些To、From、Date等字样，之后是相应的信息。

3. 事由

事由的内容只需要用名词或动名词等少数几个词，甚至一个词来概括出信息的主题。

4. 正文

正文即信息的内容，是备忘录的主要部分。写作正文时应该力求简明、确切。写作时首先应直入主题，列出最重要的信息，然后再具体说明原由、进展，提出意见和建议等，最后可以根据具体情况重申主题，或表示意愿、感谢等。需要指出的是，公司内部使用的备忘录开头无需问候语，结尾处也不需要结尾敬语和签名。写给具体某个人（例如经理写给自己的秘书）的备忘录有时需要加上称呼和签名，但一般只写名即可，不需要写姓。

许多公司都规定了备忘录的格式，标明了收信人姓名（有时候是一家公司的所有部门或某一部门所有的人）、发信人姓名、日期以及标题的位置。如果没有规定的格式，则可以使用备忘录模板或者用一张白纸来写。

二、会议记录写作要点

会议记录（Minutes of meeting）与备忘录较为相似，主要用于记录会议的程序和主要内容。它可以作为公司内部存档和历史资料以备将来查询、参考。会议记录的应用范围很广泛，如股东大会、董事会会议、高层领导会议等。此外，在外贸业务活动中，有时也需要对商务谈判做会议记录。

会议记录应忠于事实、简明扼要、抓住要点，不要带有记录人的主观看法和评论。通常情况下会议记录不是一次完成，而是在会议原始记录（如笔记、录音、简报等）的基础上整理出来的。会议记录通常在当天写好后，先由会议主持人过目再发给与会者和相关人员。

会议记录主要包括以下几个组成部分。

■ 会议名称（Title of the meeting）

会议性质、日期、时间、地点（Nature, date, time and venue of the meeting）

主持人、出席人、缺席人（moderator, present, absent）

会议内容（Content of meeting），如报告内容、发言内容、讨论事项、决议事项等（Such as report, statement, discussion, resolution etc.）

其他事项（Other topics）

下次会议日期及主要议程（Date and agenda of next meeting）

休会时间（Time of adjournment）

会议记录人签名（signature of the minutes-taker）

附件信息（Enclosure）

抄送人信息（C.C.）

同备忘录一样，有些公司也规定门会议记录的格式，相关人员可以直接采用。

第二节 备忘录及会议记录的范例讲解
(Sample Letters on Memos and Minutes of Meeting)

一、备忘录范例

范例1 预先规定格式的备忘录

MEMO

TO：＿＿＿＿＿＿＿＿

DEPT：＿＿＿＿＿＿＿ FROM：＿＿＿＿＿＿＿＿

DATE：＿＿＿＿＿＿＿ TELEPHONE：＿＿＿＿＿＿

SUBJECT：＿＿＿＿＿＿ *For your*

□APPROVAL □INFORMATION □COMMENT

范例2 自行拟定格式的备忘录（以电子邮件方式发出）

MEMO

To: Mr. Tim Evans

From: Patrick Smith

Date: May 23, 2010

Subject: Copy machine

Dear Tim,

I would like to remind you that our office is badly in need of the copy machine. I hope that you will pay attention to this problem and solve it as soon as possible.

Patrick

范例3　写给个人的备忘录

MEMO

To：James Palmer，Sales Director

From：Jane, Regional Sales Manager

Date: 23 April 2010

Subject: Survey

As requested by the Managing Director, I have done a consumer research survey concerning our products. The survey showed that the market potential for our own brand shirts could be negligible.

...

范例4　部门内部备忘录

MEMORANDUM

From: Olive, HR Manager

To: All staff

Date: June 12, 2010

Subject: Appointment of Francisco

Here we announce the appointment of Mrs. Francisco as our new Sales Manager of the Headquarter. She will be starting her job next Monday morning. There will be a small welcome party by 9:00 that day so everyone please be on time.

二、会议记录

The name and Logo of the company

Meeting Minutes

Date：   C.C.：

Location：

Present：

Next Meeting：

Ⅰ.Announcements

Ⅱ.Discussion

Ⅲ.Roundtable

Signature of the minutes-taker

Phoenix ELECTRONICS CO. LTD.

Minutes of Directors' Meeting

A directors' meeting was held on Tuesday, 22nd October 2010 at 9:00 a.m., at the

third meeting room.

Presiding: Mr. M. C. Lee, Financial manager

Present: Mr. L. K. Chen, Director; Ms. Shelly Wang, General manager;

       Mr. Tom Yang, Technical manager; Mr. L. L. Lin, Marketing manager

Absent: Mr. Ken Yu

In attendance: Willy King, consultant

1. Report

A report on the current state of company research and development was given by Director Chen.

2. Resolution

As proposed by the Chairman, the promotion for the second model of the electric drill was to be launched at the end of November, two months ahead of time. Ms. Wang seconded the motion, which was carried unanimously.

3. Selection of Manager

Mr. L. K. Chen proposed that Mr. E. A. Yang be selected as the successor to Mr. Su. The motion was seconded by Mr. Tom Yang and carried unanimously.

The meeting closed at 10.00 a.m. and the next meeting was scheduled for next week.

Signature:

Date: 22nd October 2010

范例3　中纺进出口公司会议记录

Sinotex United Import and Export Co., LTD

Address：Suite 505, Entrance B, ×× Plaza, 28 An Ding men Street

　　　　Dongcheng District, 100007 Beijing, P.R.China

电话/Tel:（+86-10）××××××××　传真/Fax:（+86-10）××××××××

Minutes of Meeting　　　　　　　　　　　**16 February 2010**

Place:　Yonghe Office

Time:　0930hs-1100hs

Date:　16 February 2010

Participants: Mr. Ralf Dach（RD）　　　Mr. Ben Guan（BG）

　　　　　　　Ms. Rae Speck（RS）　　　Ms. Wang Wuna（WWN）

　　　　　　　Mr. Pu Junli（PJL）　　　Ms. Jia Zhen（JZ）

　　　　　　　Ms. Sarah Hanberg（SH）　Ms. Lu Li（LL）

　　　　　　　Mr. Dou Xing（DX）

Results
Project management
◆ **Project website**   - Notifications of recent events should be prepared by responsible person. BG should send ***notifications*** to RD. By 26 Feb. RD should ***finalized*** the notifications.   - If the current guideline for website is not being implemented by all the projects, the head quarter will consider redesign the project website.   - DX and SH should look at the website and give fresh opinions.   ◆ **Project Improvement**   - The operational plan needs to be revised   - The ***task distributions*** within the team members and the core areas of project work shall be clearly identified. BG and PJL will draft a table of responsibility ASAP.

> - Beijing Office will discuss with ***MOFCOM*** about the issue of office space and contact Beijing office. Decision should be taken by 19 Feb. RS and JZ will follow up on this.
>
> - RS is in charge of preparing template folder and handbook. SH will assist RS in checking the folder system.
>
> - RS and BG will participate in the ***capacity building*** training.
>
> ◆ **Project budget plan**
>
> RD and BG will go over it and discuss on it.
>
> ◆ **Project Leave Management**
>
> Annual leave of project should be planned in advance but keep flexible. Business trip should be better arranged to avoid over exhausted schedule.
>
> BG will ***take 9 days*** off from 10 to 20 Mar. RD will be out of office from 26 Feb. to 4 Mar.

Jia Zhen

Project Officer

三、重要词句

1. notification通知，通告

2. task distribution任务分配

3. finalize确定，定案，定稿

4. MOFCOM：Ministry of Commerce of The People's Republic of China中国商务部

5. capacity building能力建设

6. take...days off离开……天；这里指请假、休假，也可用take leave表示。

第三节 备忘录及会议记录的实用例句
（ Useful Sentences on Memo and Minutes of Meeting ）

以下是一些常见的备忘录、会议记录例句。

1. We remind you of the necessity of...

   我们提醒您有必要……

2. Please be punctual so that we have enough time to...

   请务必准时，以便我们有足够的时间……

3. As a result, it has been decided that...

   结果是决定……

4. Further suggestions will be appreciated so that the program can be more fruitful.

   期望大家进一步提出建议以便使项目取得更加丰硕的成果。

5. It reveals the fact that...

   这表明一个事实……

6. An important part of the duties of a secretary, I think, is to do well the preparation work for the meeting.

   我认为一个秘书的重要职责之一就是做好会议的准备工作。

7. First of all, the agenda should be prepared before the meeting.

   首先，开会前要准备好议程。

8. Then you should ensure that those entitled to be present are properly informed.

   然后你要保证出席这次会议的人员都要通知到。

9. All the necessary documents and the information relevant to the meeting should be available, preferably printed and distributed before the meeting.

   所有有关会议的文件和资料都得准备妥当，最好在会议前印好并分发出去。

10. After the meeting she should type the minutes up, and keep proper records of the business transacted and resolutions passed and also implement many of the decision reached at the meeting.

会后她还要把讨论的问题和通过的决议做记录，把它打印出来，并执行在会上所做出的决定。

11. To take minutes means to make notes at a meeting so that afterwards you can write a record of what has happened.

"会议记录"是指在开会的时候记笔记，这样你可以在会后把开会的情况做个记录。

12. An informal meeting usually takes place on the spur of the moment to discuss a special point.

非正式会议通常都是为了讨论某个特殊问题而当场召开的。

13. As it was an informal meeting, I just made a short report.

因为那是一个非正式会议，所以我只写了一个简短纪要。

练习题

1. 将如下会议记录译成中文并添加会议记录的题头

Project management
◆ **Project Improvement**   - Project team staff should prepare written hand-over report before taking days off. Miss Liu will contact the head quarter to get the debriefing checklist and prepare report on how to hand over documents and tasks.   - Project will not outsource translation work to external agency in the future. Exceptional case for outsourcing should be proved by the director. All the staff is considered as the internal project translation team.   - Ms. Jia will print out the filing system for the director and collect his suggestions.   - Rest of the project team will also participate the training in August. Mr. Li will develop methods to evaluate training impact.   - BG should call the head quarter for the new format for the report and draft the report to Mofcom by 10 Apr. RS will translate afterwards.

- PMO should develop feedback recording form for the use of result-based monitoring.

- SH will be in charge of the website promotion and search engine optimization.

2. 阅读如下备忘录并译成中文

From: HGW

To: Department managers

Date: 21/4/2009

Subject: In-service English classes

1. From Monday, 8 May, English classes will be held in the training Center (Room 317) . There will be two groups: intermediate level (8:30–10:00) and advanced level (10:30–12:00) . Please encourage your staff to attend one of the sessions. All teaching materials will be provided but students will be expected to do homework and preparation outside working hours.

2. Please send me the names of all interested staff by noon on Wednesday, 26 April. They will be given an informed oral test during the first week in May so that we can decide which of the classes is best for them.

3. The size of each class will be limited to 12 participants.

3. 根据如下内容起草一个备忘录并拟定一个题头

你是一家国际大公司的人力资源部经理。你刚刚任命萨莉·琼克（Sally Jocker）女士为公司总部的销售经理。请你给总部的全体员工写一份字数为40~50字的备忘录，主要内容包括：

——宣布对萨莉·琼克女士的任命；

——说明她开始工作的具体时间；

——要求总部员工准备欢迎她。

参考文献

胡鉴明. 商务英语函电. 北京：中国商务出版社，2004

尹小莹，杨润辉. 外贸英语函电. 第四版. 西安：西安交通大学出版社，2008

檀文茹，徐静珍. 外贸函电. 北京：中国人民大学出版社，2003

考特兰，博韦等. 博韦商务沟通. 喆儒译. 北京：中国人民大学出版社，2009

基蒂·O·洛克. 商务与管理沟通. 北京：机械工业出版社，2006

黎海滨. 现代英语应用文写作指南. 上海：上海大学出版社，2004

葛萍，周维家. 外贸英语函电. 上海：复旦大学出版社，2007

吴思乐. 外经贸英语信函写作. 北京：机械工业出版社，2010

柴智秀. 世纪商务英语：函电与单证. 第二版. 大连：大连理工出版社，2008

教辅产品及教师会员申请表

申请教师姓名			
所在学校		所在院系	
联系电话		电子邮件地址	
通信地址			
教授课程名称		学生人数	
您的授课对象	本科□ 研究生□ MBA□ EMBA□ 高职高专□ 其他□		
教材名称		作者	
书号		订购册数	
您对该教材的评价			
您教授的其他课程名称		学生人数	
准备选用或正在使用的教材 （教材名称 出版社）			
您的研究方向		是否对教材翻译或改编有兴趣？	是□ 否□
您是否对编写教材感兴趣？		是□ 否□	
您推荐的教材是：＿＿＿＿＿＿＿＿＿＿＿＿＿＿＿＿＿＿＿＿＿			
推荐理由：＿＿＿＿＿＿＿＿＿＿＿＿＿＿＿＿＿＿＿＿＿			

为确保教辅资料仅为教师获得，请将此申请表加盖院系公章后传真或寄回给我们，谢谢！

教师签名：

院/ 系办公室公章

地　　址：北京市崇文区龙潭路甲3号翔龙大厦B06室
　　　　　北京普华文化发展有限公司
邮　　编：100061
传　　真：（010）67120121
读者热线：（010）67129879　67129872转818/205
网　　址：http://www.puhuabook.com.cn
邮购电话：（010）67129872转818
编辑信箱：daixinmei@puhuabook.com